A Father and Son

Walking Experience

The French and North Caminos

Dr. Ruben Barron

ISBN 978-1-63844-487-9 (paperback)
ISBN 978-1-63844-488-6 (digital)

Christian Faith Publishing, Inc.
832 Park Avenue
Meadville, PA 16335
www.christianfaithpublishing.com

Printed in the United States of America

Contents

Acknowledgments

———— ✐ ————

Two people, more than anyone else, made the Camino experience possible for me. Without the full support of my wife, Socorro, an eighty-five-day pilgrimage is not feasible. Her encouraging assurance gave me the peace of mind to be truly away and in the moment without any need to worry about her. After fifty years together, our marriage can more readily shift possibilities into reality. The one question that never entered my mind (and which I never understood) friends posed to her was, "What will you do while Ruben is away?" Actually, she did fine and so did the plants she tended and the home repairs I had postponed. I am grateful to her and most fortunate.

Sometimes, it takes another person's vision to prompt us to act, and Father Mike Hanifin's dream of walking to the holy site he had visited by bus was the impetus for me to walk the Camino. His goal enticed my son and I to join his small group in 2014, and while we ended up walking the French Camino at different paces, I am grateful for the seed that he planted. It continues to grow. Over the years that I have known him, Father Mike has explored many fruitful paths. I am glad the Camino is one of them.

I am particularly blessed that my son, Ruben Daniel, was my walking partner during two very different Caminos. His prints are in all the shared activities of washing clothes, Cola Cao breaks, finding *albergues*, playing gin rummy and foosball and particularly doing long, endless walks. The time we shared touched my heart deeply as it was easily the most quality time we have ever spent together. I know it was not easy to take the time from work but a wise decision! The Camino helped me to reconnect with Mijo (Spanish for son) and appreciate his qualities of reaching out to others and remaining steadfast despite harsh obstacles. Thank you, Mijo, for sharing the Camino with me and for the priceless gift of time.

The Camino is a metaphor for life and at the heart of it are the people who share it with us. Our Southern California fellow travelers on the first Camino include Father Mike Hanifin, Nancy Sink, Pablo Mejia, Brad Heavey, Cathy Zimmer, Loretta Alonso, and Daniel Cruz. We shared the Camino beginning with our monthly luncheons during our year of preparation and at various points along the way. Like life, we each did the Camino our own way. My memories of this special time include all of you and Ed Baluyot, our helpful friend, who at the end did not receive medical release to join us.

Introduction

The Camino de Santiago de Compostela refers to the one-thousand-plus-year-old tradition of making one's way to the city of Santiago in Northwest Spain where the apostle St. James's bones lie today. Although the trek has multiple points of origin and means of travel, the most popular is the five-hundred-mile path from Saint-Jean-Pied-de-Port, France, known as the French Camino or its Spanish name. The Frances takes you over the Pyrenees Mountains through rich farmland with some of the world's best wines, beautiful and historically significant cities, and hundreds of small villages. It is in the ancient towns, each with its own central plaza and old church, where one feels a close connection to generations of earlier travelers and native hosts. Here, you meet friendly down-to-earth people whose welcoming spirit cuts through centuries of time.

There is something deeply primitive about walking. It is the most natural thing we do as humans, and it is a fundamental desire and need we share with other creatures. Starting with the first shaky step a smiling child takes, we are always happiest moving, even after falling. For centuries, people of all shapes and shades, sizes and ages have walked the Camino de Santiago: The Way.

Although many people walk the Camino for nonreligious reasons, today, it is one of the three most popular Christian pilgrimage sites along with Jerusalem and Rome. The Camino de Santiago (Saint James) de Compostela (field of stars) refers to a destination, not an origin. There are several caminos (paths) leading to Santiago and ways to do them. Some people walk, carry their own backpack, and stay in hostels. Others may walk but carry only water/snacks and pay to have their gear transported. Still others bike their way through or only do a portion of the Camino, returning years later to do the rest. Walking a hundred kilometers (sixty-two miles) qualifies for an official certificate of completion: a Compostela.

My forty-something son and I experienced our first Camino together on the Camino Frances in 2014. It was a highly well-planned endeavor that paid off by reaching our destination in thirty-one days at an average walking pace close to sixteen miles a day. Afterward, we were both spent and energized feeling a great need to slowly savor the wonderful adventure without any thought of returning.

Four years later, however, we found ourselves making plans to return. This time, we would walk the slightly longer, cooler, and more difficult North Camino (Camino Norte). During the eight hundred years that the Moors occupied Spain, this far northern route was the only safe pathway to Santiago. Today, only 6 percent of those who complete the Camino use this "original" route.

Unlike our earlier experience of ending our pilgrimage in Santiago, we decided to walk an additional ninety kilometers to Finisterre (the end of the world). In olden times, people walked beyond Santiago to Finisterre from where they took a scallop shell home with them to venerate their journey. It is a long-standing tradition that we wanted to honor.

Walking the two Caminos with my son has been highly healing. One uncovers great freedom when relying on your own two feet to carry all of your essential belongings, not knowing exactly where you will eat or sleep that night, and being where you never have before and likely never will again. The immensity of the Camino experience makes it easier for pilgrims to soften, if not surrender, their individual will and let God lead the way.

The Camino is a gift of quality time to contemplate, to be alone with one's thoughts, and to listen without the usual stream of noise. This aspect of the Camino is so special to me that I refused to take any technology with me on either trek. It forced me to reach out to locals for directions and led to many pleasant exchanges. The decision highlighted the human dimension of the Camino experience, and I remain deeply grateful to my Spanish brothers and sisters who kept me on the right path.

How we live our lives reflect how we approach the Camino. If we are used to "controlling the agenda" at home, the Camino may be particularly unsettling and a potential source for growth. Spanish hosts use the refrain, "Tourists demand, pilgrims are grateful." In describing my intense physical and mental preparation for the Camino to a friend, she asked if I was leaving room for surprises. What an astute observation!

On the Camino, I read a sign suggesting that we do not do the Camino (just as we do not do life) but rather that the Camino does us. This was one of many helpful reminders to relax and enjoy the present moment without great concern for everything around and beyond. I needed the nudge as I am inclined to rely on a sure bet.

Along the way, I spoke with hikers on just another long challenging trail admittedly with no regard or interest in spiritual matters. I also met Mr. Chin whose voice, demeanor, and very being seemed mystical. Many of us seemed to fall somewhere in between. The main difference between hiking, vacationing, and pilgrimage is that the latter is an inward voyage where no encounter is without meaning. Staying focused on doing a pilgrimage is not easy when your body aches and your mind is fixated on distance covered and keeping safe.

Before setting off, Mijo and I made some fundamental travel decisions. In solidarity with generations of previous pilgrims without modern services, we undertook a traditional pilgrimage on foot, carrying our own gear, and staying in basic *albergues* (hostels). Digital television, large showers, and soft beds seemed out of step with the mindset of a pilgrim.

Prayer of Trust

My Lord God, I have no idea where I am going.
I do not see the road ahead of me.
I cannot know for certain where it will end.
Nor do I really know myself, and the fact that
I think that I am following your will does
not mean that I am actually doing so.
But I believe that the desire to please you
does in fact please you.
And I hope that I will never do anything apart
from that desire.
And I know that if I do this you will lead me by the
right road though I may know nothing about it.
Therefore, will I trust you always though
I may seem to be lost and in the shadow of death.
I will not fear, for you are ever with me, and
you will never leave me to face my perils alone.
(Thomas Merton)

Care for a Walk?

Father Mike's email invitation to a conversation about doing the Camino de Santiago de Compostela was one I'd normally decline. Out of shape at sixty-seven years old with no hiking experience, the idea of taking a series of long walks in a foreign country was not particularly appealing. I like to exercise at the gym and play some tennis, and I like the outdoors. That was about the only thing that helped me show up and not feel completely out of place.

My relationship with Father Mike tipped the scale. He had always shown very sound judgment and pointed me in the right direction more than once and, at times, toward a path not of my choosing or within my sphere of imagination. I decided to join the meeting thinking I might work up the courage to walk for a week or two and perhaps manage to meander, say, fifty miles. Even that seemed intense; the last time I walked more than a few miles, I was a young soldier! Out of seemingly nowhere, "my wife needs me at home" settled in my mind as I thought about the meeting.

Such was my mindset and indifference a year before embarking on the Camino. It was obviously something I would have never done of my own free will. The wall of resistance was firm but about to collapse as I became more open to new possibilities. Allowing myself to explore fresh ground gave way to dramatic change. The first Camino lesson started at home as a reminder that we do not always control what happens to us, and if we are open to the unknown, we may be astonished.

My adult son happened to be visiting from Los Angeles and joined his mother and me as we made our way to San Clemente.

The Camino was still shredded in mystery. I had browsed through some literature and seen the movie *The Way* where Martin Sheen, as a result of his son's death on the Camino, ends up taking his place. I had no compelling reason to delve any deeper.

The exploratory conversation and creation of calendar options I anticipated never materialized. Instead, an itinerary with beginning and ending dates was shared showing thirty-three days of walking between twelve and twenty miles a day for a total of five hundred miles. We would start in Saint-Jean-Pied-de-Port, France, less than one hundred miles from Lourdes and end up in the famous Cathedral of Santiago de Compostela. Father Mike had done his homework, and the commitment was huge!

People close to me know that I don't make big decisions on the spot if I have time to consider the implications. On this occasion, I blurted out an interest in doing the whole Camino Frances on our way home after the meeting. One good bombshell deserves another, and my son added that he would join me. I don't know what prompted his reaction or mine, but it unleashed energy and determination that we could channel into a whole year of preparation.

Voices of Experience

Looking forward, a year seems a long time to prepare for a trip, but that is not the case for a Camino pilgrimage. When our temperament is deeply entrenched in the conveniences of our modern consumer culture, it takes time and work to accept crowded sleeping quarters, a small hard bunk, and public showers with intermittent running water. It is not easy to transition from a leisurely life in Southern California to carrying one's belongings across a foreign land on aching feet. I was determined not to simply experience a long hike, which I could do in the Pacific Crest Trail or other local site. I wanted to prepare for the unique privilege to connect with millions of pilgrims from all over the world walking the same route over thousands of years—some for religious reasons others for the exercise or simply because they could. The challenge I envisioned was no more physical than mental. I began my preparation by learning about the Camino through books, videos, and experienced pilgrims.

Under Father Mike's direction, I coordinated monthly luncheons in a local restaurant to hear from invited guests with Camino experience. Group attendance was open and normally drew a dozen hopeful individuals who grew more excited as time progressed. Of those who attended the informative sessions, five eventually booked Camino flights together. Others decided against going or postponed their plans. Two newcomers joined our group just before we departed. The presentations provided us with valuable information giving us a chance to ask questions and clarify misinformation. With each monthly meeting, the group grew more excited about doing the Camino as individuals made informed personal decisions.

Through the interactive luncheons, we heard from couples as well as from men and women who had done the Camino by themselves. Some shared lists of gear they took, mentioned things they forgot to carry, and offered helpful advice on essentials like taking trekking poles and breaking in the equipment while still at home. Most took a communication device such as cellphone or iPad. We gained good insights about the types of facilities we could expect and the costs involved.

The presenters shared rich commonalities from their particular perspectives but also a variety of personal stories such as the entrepreneur who redid the Camino to fit his personality, the priest who, while on pilgrimage in India, casually moseyed over to do the Camino Frances, and a lady in her seventies who did the Camino five times—that's 2,500 miles and many pairs of boots. We learned about the type of food to expect, weather conditions, and sleeping quarters along with other vital information.

Our lunch guests were gracious and generous with their stories giving us opportunities to distill from them those most palpable to our own personality, desires, and expectations. My son's work and travel distance prevented him from participating, so whenever possible, I related the main points. One which I came to understand more personally on the Camino was that people approach the Camino as they do life. The mindset manifests itself in the daily tasks and decisions such as where to lodge, walking pace, rest periods, laundry habits, and interactions with fellow pilgrims and indigenous people. You do not become a new person just by showing up.

Various luncheon speakers and writers emphasized the importance of traveling light, and I made that my mantra. The concept resonated on multiple levels. Learning that some people get rid of extra baggage soon after arriving at their starting point on the Camino is wasteful. Still, others are forced to quit the Camino, in the early stages, because of physical trauma and injury, or they uncover complications after completing the Camino. These ill-fated experiences helped me make decisions to protect my body. I committed myself to carry no more than the recommended 10 percent of my body weight. Most of us are surrounded by "stuff" and have a very hard time nearing the suggested standard of weight to carry.

Are You Walking Alone?

As a Roman Catholic, my interest in the historical roots of the Camino came easily. Reading about the valiant travels of the original apostles, their influence throughout the known world, and the gallant finality of their lives was fascinating. St. James (Santiago) had no less an inspirational life than other apostles. I enjoyed delving into the celebrated history of Spain and revisiting some of my old books from university classes on its historical development as well as its great literature. I had not given much thought to the fact that I had been calling friends saints for years. I had assumed Santiago to translate to James without realizing that the Spanish version holds both saint and James within it.

My initial focus on the Camino's long history and Spanish culture changed to preparing myself physically ten weeks before departure. Apparently, what I needed and lacked most was hiking experience not only to learn technique and condition my body but also to break in my new shoes and use the essentials including backpack, water container, and poles. I needed to acquire experience in and learn how to pack correctly, how to think of water while hiking, and the proper use of poles in different walking conditions. I was even given advice on how to tie my shoelaces so that they stay in place without risk of loosening. In these areas, I was starting from scratch.

On the initial hike at home, I felt like a kid on the first day of school—brandishing new shoes and clothes, excited about the mystery of what lay ahead, and wheezy about the new surroundings. My excitement plunged swiftly as I stood numbly gazing at a huge sign at the entrance of the state park. Beside the big images of threatening rattle snakes, fierce mountain lions, and coyotes was a stern warning not to walk alone. I felt like someone had just burst my bubble. It was not exactly the welcome I had anticipated.

After some dry soul-searching and in spite of the caveats, I set out that sunny morning in a new direction. Two thoughts filled my mind: just how rampant and dangerous are the animals, and is it really unwise for me to hike alone? Whistling and singing seemed a good way to scare wild life, and I soon found myself doing that every time I approached large vegetation near the trail. The awkward practice broke off when, rounding a bend singing at the top of my voice, a puzzled hiker asked if I needed help.

The value of using two poles to hike became most evident on rocky and steep trails. Claims that the poles provide 25 percent relief on the body are probably not exaggerated. When you consider the toll on your feet from long daily walks, you want to do everything possible to lighten the load. The collapsible poles quickly became treasured items. I found them helpful not only on unleveled terrain but also on flat paths. However carefully we may fill the backpack (with heavier items on the bottom and nearest your back), body movements shift the contents and throw it off balance. Two lightweight poles are indispensable for the uneven hiking conditions of the Camino.

By the third day of hiking, I was no longer fixated on being attacked by wild animals. Suppressing that distress helped me to realize that I was not walking alone. During those very hot summer days of strenuous physical activity, I discovered a deep serenity in walking and found calmness in the solitude that nature provides. Instinctively, my focus turned to my immediate environment that increasingly included God. I started looking forward to the hikes and feeling incomplete when I skipped a day. Whenever a blister appeared, I laid off hiking to give my feet adequate time to replenish soft skin with a harden layer more fitting for the Camino.

While training, my son and I had a chance to hike together, and it taught me a valuable lesson. On my own, I had become comfortable hiking at a quick pace to build up my stamina and move out of the hot sun. My focus had become a hurried walk from point A to

B. He introduced an important element to my routine. Now, I had someone to chat with who was in no great hurry to arrive anywhere. He did not mind taking breaks along the way and even stopped to loosen his shoelaces and rest his feet. The experience helped me to consider different ways of hiking and prepared me to anticipate how we may approach the Camino together.

It is hard to overstate the importance of physical preparation before departure. The severely blistered feet I saw on the first day on the Camino, and pretty much throughout the entire journey, would have kept me from completing it. In fact, some people are not able to continue after the first day or the first week. My son was one of the lucky ones who, having to walk on blistered feet from day one on the Camino, never lost hope and finished much stronger than when he started. As in life, the Camino is not about where we start or the falls along the way but our commitment to get up, heal the wounds, and move forward.

Reading the history of the Camino helped shape the way to approach it and in making decisions about what to take. I envisioned early pilgrims on an ambiguous journey coping with the inherent dangers and none of the modern conveniences. Their courage and faith paved the way for future generations of pilgrims. However small a measure, I wanted to honor their spirit. That became the primary reason for deciding against using technology, earplugs, or pain medication. I even left my watch at home. A secondary consideration for traveling light was avoiding the clamor and clutter of the modern world. Noise was the last thing I wanted to haul for five hundred miles.

Once we renewed our nearly expired passports (it took about four months to complete the process), Mijo and I each bought $300 euros from local banks and set up a special account for expenses during the Camino. I felt good knowing that if I lost the only debit card I carried, the account was purposely bare for my wife to replenish from home only as needed. As it turned out, the practice of carrying some euros along with one debit card worked out well as there were plenty of places where we could use our cards to draw funds.

A Blessing from Bishop Kevin Vann

--- ❧ ---

B efore departing, my wife and I hosted an evening prayer service and potluck at home. In addition to our friends doing the Camino, we invited the monthly luncheon speakers to thank them for sharing their personal stories. The monthly workshops to prepare for the Camino allowed us to learn from each other, share resources, and establish friendships. The prayer service where the bishop would send us on our way was the final celebration of the year's activities.

Father Mike organized the prayer service and copied a beautiful Camino prayer for each of us to meditate upon during the journey. Some of us pasted the prayer on the guidebook that we carried to reflect on it while making our daily hiking plans. It was wonderful to have our diocesan spiritual leader, Bishop Keith Vann, lead us in prayer and give the group a special blessing for the pilgrimage. One of the couples was celebrating their wedding anniversary and received a blessing from the bishop. We decided that it was important to gather again for a time of gratitude after the Camino.

I shared a slightly revised schedule for the Camino that called for walking every day except Sundays. The five-hundred-mile trek was divided into thirty-three stages, each twelve to twenty miles long, with the goal of completing a stage a day. We allotted ourselves a few contingency days including flight times, days of worship, and free periods totaling forty-three days from August 26 to October 7, 2014. We chose to walk after students had returned to school while avoiding extreme heat or cold conditions.

The itinerary served as a general guide. Outside of the flight schedule, the remaining details would evolve. Group-walking pilgrimages deal with too many variables such as health issues, individual walking pace, weather conditions, and personal inclinations that no timetable can predict. Allowing mental space for the unexpected enables people to enjoy their time walking regardless of the challenges that evolve along the way while to trying to assert one's will only produces frustration.

The Prayer of Faba

Although I may have travelled all the roads, crossed mountains and valleys from east to west, if I have not discovered the freedom to be myself, I have arrived nowhere.

Although I may have shared all of my possessions with people of other languages and cultures; made friends with pilgrims of a thousand paths, or shared *albergues* with saints and princes, if I am not capable of forgiving my neighbor tomorrow, I have arrived nowhere.

Although I may have carried my pack from beginning to end and waited for every pilgrim in need of encouragement, or given my bed to one who arrived later than I, given my bottle of water in exchange for nothing; if upon returning to my home and work, I am not able to create brotherhood or make happiness, peace and unity, I have arrived nowhere.

Although I may have had food and water each day, and enjoyed a roof and shower every night; or may have had my injuries well attended, if I have not discovered in all that the love of God, I have arrived nowhere.

Although I may have seen all the monuments and contemplated the best sunsets; although I may have learned a greeting in every language;

or tried the clean water from every fountain; if I have not discovered who is the author of so much free beauty and so much peace, I have arrived nowhere.

If from today I do not continue walking on your path, searching for and living according to what I have learned; if from today I do not see in every person, friend or foe a companion on the Camino; if from today I cannot recognize God, the God of Jesus of Nazareth as the one God of my life, I have arrived nowhere. (Rebecca Gallo)

Travel Light

———— ❦ ————

It was time to sift through the main points from our luncheon speakers coupled with our individual vision of walking the Camino and put it to practical use. What seemed most important to me was to travel light. I dreaded hurting myself for lack of attention or missing out on a fulfilling Camino because of my negligence. Whatever it took, I was ready to cooperate, and while it was easier to focus on the physical aspects of that goal, I didn't want to ignore the psychological and spiritual pieces.

When you understand that you will rely on what you carry during the entire time in Europe, it is wise to pack the essentials. When you realize that you must carry what you pack, your definition of essentials changes. The Camino is not a solitary road without services. In a pinch, you are likely to find what you need and especially medical supplies. The prevailing attitude on the Camino is one of service. In need, you will find your item in a store or someone will give it to you. So it is more important to pack wisely than liberally. That, however, is much easier said than done. We are a society driven toward acquiring stuff: we want the latest, more of it and now.

In my readings, I came across good advice about drinking a lot of fluids and staying hydrated as a means of preventing blisters and, I'm sure, a whole host of other ailments. From my own experience on the Camino, it's great counsel. Mijo and I both bought a three-liter bladder rather than the smaller one- or two-liters alternatives. This is the one area where you need to don't want to go small. I'm not used to drinking water straight from the tap but had no problem doing so throughout the Camino.

Traveling light suggests making right choices and not simply reducing weight. Yet some choices are not as clear as others. One of the early key decisions was between hiking shoes or boots that offer greater ankle support and protection from rain. I opted for shoes and refused the inserts that the sales person suggested on the grounds that I would be introducing a new element that I may not need. That turned out to be a good choice for me. Mijo who chose to wear boots with inserts for greater protection against injury was also fine with his decision. I was taught to tie my laces using two different means to avoid slippage. It worked. Mijo made no changes in this regard. He didn't mind checking his boots often.

Aside from getting your body ready for long hikes, the most critical feature of training at home is using the footwear to be certain it is right for you. I'm sure I walked over three hundred miles at home which is more than enough to know that I had bought the right shoes and wool socks. One of our speakers had emphasized breathability and durability aspects of hiking gear which certainly applies to shoes and socks. The wrong socks can keep moisture and prime your feet for blisters. Interestingly, there are walkers intent on keeping their feet moist and others dry. You need to do what works for your own body. Three years of military service taught me to keep my feet dry, and that continues to work well for me.

I was concerned to learn that some people fail to train sufficiently, injure themselves, and are forced to discontinue their Camino plans. Accidents can and do happen even among experienced hikers. But there is a way to minimize risk, and that's to prepare well. Some people who run often or work out daily at the gym assume readiness for the Camino. While their good conditioning will certainly help, it is important to match the type of preparation exercise with the actual activity being undertaken. It sounds obvious, but it is an issue. The best way to prepare to hike long distances carrying a full backpack is to hike long distances in varied (not only flat) surfaces.

I began hiking two or three times a week without a full pack for six to eight miles. I did that for about two weeks. I gradually started carrying more weight and walking longer distances until doing twelve to fifteen miles with a full backpack in very uneven mountain terrain. A friend suggested hiking three consecutive days for conditioning. It was a really good observation that reflects the demands made on the body and mind on the Camino. The practice prepared me to the point where the training regimen became more difficult than the actual Camino.

"In you, not on you" as it relates to water is another crucial piece of advice that helps avoid injury. I carried the equivalent of seven pounds of water easily—the single heaviest item in my backpack. In the container, the water was a useless liability. In my body, it lightened the load and kept me hydrated. I learned not to wait until I was thirsty to take a drink but to drink constantly. I take an extra sixteen-ounce water container with electrolyte replacements that I drink on every hike. Carrying only the snacks that you consume for the day and not accumulating keep them and you fresh.

The first concrete sign that our little group of seven was approaching the Camino differently came at the Los Angeles airport in the form of bulky backpacks. My son is six feet four inches; I was the second biggest person in the group. Ours were the two smallest packs, and we carried everything we needed but nothing extra. We limited ourselves to two sets of all clothing. I broke my trifold toothbrush and took only one third with me; my journal consisted of ten single lose pages. We were all able to hand carry our equipment except for, our young friend, Daniel. He joined us late and took a different flight. Daniel checked in his gear in Los Angeles and lost it for a couple of days.

From Madrid, we took a small shuttle to Pamplona where a van that Ed Baluyot had reserved for us was waiting. Making our way out of the airport was a uniformed man holding up a sign that read, "Barron." It had the effect of saying, "You are not a total stranger, welcome." From Pamplona, we had a pleasant and inexpensive hour drive to Saint-Jean-Pied-de-Port without checkpoints between national borders.

What my son and I took are the following:

- Hat with flaps to protect the neck
- Headlamp for early morning walking
- Headband (I didn't need one but my son who sweats profusely did)

- Two long-sleeved shirts and two shorts
- Silk liner, sleeping bag not needed
- One set of zipper attachments for shorts
- Rainproof jacket with hood, no poncho needed
- Two sets of light underwear
- Two sets of wool socks
- One pair of hiking shoes (he took boots) and an extra set of laces, which I used
- One pair of sandals with toe support
- Nail clippers
- Laundry wash and body soap, leaves not recommended
- Small chamois towel for shower use
- Two collapsible trekking poles
- Forty-five-liter backpack
- Moleskin
- Three liter water bladder
- Ninety servings of electrolyte powder and a sixteen-ounce water bottle
- Lip gloss, floss, and toothpaste
- Small toothbrush (broke mine to make it extra small)
- Pen and ten loose sheets of paper (wrote back to back with no margins)
- John Brierley's *A Pilgrim's Guide to the Camino de Santiago*
- Batteries for my hearing aids
- Small bag for toiletries (I created a hook for hanging and that helped)

The French Camino

Expensive Salad

The early afternoon arrival in Saint-Jean-Pied-de-Port gave us time to find the tourist office and acquire Camino passports (Credencial de Peregrino) for a small fee. These long folding documents are stamped wherever one lodges and even coffee shops and churches provide the service. Once the Camino is complete, the passport shows proof of one's journey and entitles the bearer to an official sealed certificate (Compostela) showing both the starting date and site and date of completion plus total kilometers covered. Another option is to order a certificate while still at home and take it with you on the Camino.

Settling in the first night of our arrival in France was a bit of a quandary. We are jet lagged, tired, and in a foreign land. People around us are speaking in varied languages. Many are hauling hiking gear and seem lost. Our first priority is to find lodging. Looking around, we join a long line of longing pilgrims where French-speaking volunteers refer us to possible lodging sites in this beautiful Basque village. Most of us carried a copy of the John Brierley book containing detail maps of *albergue* (basic sleeping quarters with two-tier bunk beds) locations but found it hard to follow it on this occasion.

After some random searches, we stumble across a comfortable place to stay for fifteen euros each, giving us a taste of our budding adventure. The sign to the office is not clearly marked, and once there, no one is around to check us in. A message at the entrance instructs us to find a bunk and pay later. Luckily, accommodations are plentiful, and the men and women in our group claim separate rooms. Later, we learn that neither checking yourself in nor sleeping separately is the norm.

After washing and hanging our clothes to dry, my son and I locate an outdoor coffee shop to relax with Daniel. Soon, the rest of the group joins us, still trying to shake off the jet lag. As the group begins to disperse, Mijo and I decide on dinner at a large casual restaurant under some trees with a view of the street. The weather is nice, and the site seems like a good place to continue our acclimation.

I thought fifteen euros for bunking was high and study the menu prices closely before settling on a couple of wholesome salads. When we get our check with the large number sixty-seven encircled, I'm puzzled. Sixty-seven euros for a couple of salads! Even with a sandwich and drink, it is just short of a hundred dollars for a meal of vegetables. Without an itemized check and in broken French, I motion the waitress over and try to point out her mistake. After some noticeable effort on both our parts, she finally understands my concern and bursts out laughing. Evidently, we were sitting on table sixty-seven. It seems like every employee was alerted to our little faux pas pausing in their hurried tracks for a glance at table sixty-seven. Pilgrims!

Blister Girl

I t takes only one night to realize that when others sleeping next to you in close quarters awaken, you do the same. No matter how delicately lights flash on or how smoothly people shuffle around, no snooze button will save you. By four thirty that first crisp morning, we assemble in the kitchen trying to get our bearings. Having retrieved our washed laundry, filled our water vessels from the small kitchen sink, and acquired snacks for a climb of almost five thousand feet, we are ready for our first hike in Europe.

Once everyone is settled in the small room, Father Mike reminds us to turn on our headlamps and leads us in prayer. Earlier talks of taking two days to complete the difficult first leg are dismissed. With the adrenaline flowing, no one suggests that we cut the route in half, and we set out to walk over eighteen miles, adjusted for climb. We opt to travel the scenic and strenuous Route de Napoleon (Pyrenees) across the French-Spanish border into Roncesvalles in the providence of Navarra. I already like the adventurous spirit of our group.

The route from France to Spain contains some of the most stunning views of the entire Camino Frances—long winding paths with horses and sheep grazing on lush green rolling hills. It is one of the most demanding legs of the entire Camino, and hikers are advised to exercise great caution, especially downhill at the end of the day. Many pilgrims skip this stage to avoid the steep climbs and descents and start their walk on the Spanish side. The exceptional beauty in this area, however, is well worth the extra effort.

The early hikes are good indicators of the demands of the Camino. People quickly learn the extent of their readiness and how to approach the Camino. We see several people on the side of the road on the initial hike nursing their sore feet and developing blisters. Busy people with little free time to train or those who lack the right equipment face the same conditions as everyone else. From day one, talk of blisters becomes the predominant topic. This is actually quite helpful as people begin to share material resources and experiential knowledge. Hikers with medical backgrounds offer their support and everyone else their sympathy. Fellow pilgrims come to know a young lady as blister girl. At various times and places, we would hear someone call out, "Blister girl, how are you today?"

On the first hike, one of my hearing aids unexpectedly gives out. It is annoying and made worse by my inability to repair it. The beauty of the Camino, along with the physical suffering of fellow pilgrims, sway me from self-pity and lead me to focus on the fact that I can still hear from the other ear. How our responses shape us is illustrated by a privileged man who was traumatized by being left in a confessional booth by himself as a young child for a short time. Another man recollected being leased by his poor parents to make ends meet and having to live away from his family as a young child. He said nothing about being traumatized and showed no signs of it.

My son had not had time to train and break in his equipment, and although he was strongly focused on the end target "one step at a time" as he puts it, I offer to trade backpacks. He carries a good size camera, our sole luxury, making his backpack slightly larger and heavier. Thinking he needs a few days to acclimate, I suggest exchanging again on the seventh day to which he readily agrees.

My only fall on the Camino occurs in the Pyrenees when I do not hear a car approaching around a bend and step back suddenly into a grassy vacuum. My son's big backpack softens the blow and probably prevents a more serious injury, although I do not recall being grateful at the time. Hauling his hefty camera turns out to be a good tactic. Walking each day close together enables him to reach easily into my gear, without having to unload the backpack, and use the camera on the trail. I offer to keep the camera the entire Camino.

Before reaching Pamplona, on our third hike, our little group has already dispersed. We are all walking at our distinct comfortable stride, which is quite natural and to be expected. The mistake we made was not taking sufficient time to share our individual desires and expectations with each other. It became a source of confusion with some feeling abandoned or not supported. If reaching some understanding of how to approach the Camino together between two individuals is important, it becomes more so with multiple people involved.

My son and I continue to walk together as we attempt to find a pace that works for both of us. I am having trouble adjusting to his backpack and keep tweaking the straps without good results. I am facing equipment issues that I had already worked out during the weeks of training at home and did not realize how comfortable I had already grown with my own gear. It was an opportunity to empathize with others adjusting to so many changes. Unfortunately, I chose to dwell on my own troubles. I'm sure I complained more than was necessary or helpful.

Around me, people suffer physically and even adjusting to the food, language, and culture. "Why isn't more English spoken instead of so much Spanish?" "Why are the *albergue* hosts so insensitive to the long lines of tired people waiting to check in as they patiently greet each person signing their roster?" These circumstances help me shift perspective and eventually find myself expressing gratitude for the hearing aid that still works and the ability to carry a heavier backpack than I had expected.

Early Camino lessons were good reminders that we had left Kansas. The much different environment would continue to challenge us but also provide opportunities for growth and self-discovery. The biggest blind spot was assuming that our high hopes fueled by invigorating settings would automatically engender new insights. We had inner work to do. The pilgrim's task was just beginning, as the story of a troubled man ditching Los Angeles for a better place in Santa Fe illustrates. He asks a friend what people are like in Santa Fe, and the friend, in turn, asks him to describe people in Los Angeles. "Well, they're selfish and inconsiderate" came the reply, to which his friend responds, "You'll probably find people in Santa Fe selfish and inconsiderate."

Missing Technology and Missing People

— ❦ —

As group members transition into the mindset of a foreign pilgrim in our own distinct way, our individual approach and response to the Camino is birthing and is no small reflection of seven distinct personalities. Hiking through the crowded streets of Pamplona, famous for its annual running of the bulls, we come across hundreds of joggers and temporarily closed streets. There is a big wedding party outside the local church with colorful musicians, and I stop there as others window shop. Later, I hear that a pilgrim, standing with his heavy backpack among the hordes of people, was tipped over by two men who escaped with his wallet. I don't know how common this type of incident is. I never saw anything like it except when our group lost some technology.

Only three days into the pilgrimage, we have already crossed six rivers and as many bridges, some dating to Roman times. I borrow a phone to make group reservations for the next day in the city of Cizur Menor where we stay in an *albergue* with several smaller rooms as opposed to the more common single huge room. Speaking Spanish helps, but many volunteers at the typical *albergues* or hotel personnel speak English.

On this first Saturday evening in Cizur Menor, we experience a power shortage and next morning discover missing technology and money. In piecing together the night's events, it seems somebody was seen or heard going through pilgrims' possessions in the deep night. Mijo and I carried minimal luxuries (a well-hidden camera) and slept each night with our valuables in our pants' pockets. We did not suffer any losses.

Our group's spirit is clearly dampened. As we leave the *albergue*, Brad and Cathy remain behind to deal with their missing cell phones, which were never recovered. Two other members of our party had taken a taxi the day before and appear to be struggling physically today. By the fourth day of hiking, we are clearly immersed in the Camino and increasingly losing sight of each other.

The bigger cities with typical urban distractions make it hard to find the scallop shells that guide hikers on the Camino. The shell's grooves, extending from a single point, represent the various Camino routes and their common destination. As the symbol of the Camino de Santiago, the blue or yellow shell is seen on wood posts, rocks, or the side of buildings in rural communities. The metropolitan shells are often a softer color, although more elaborate, and embedded unto sidewalks, streets, or on high walls. Many pilgrims hang hard shells on their backpacks which can be heavy and noisy. A better choice is to sew or glue a fabric shell.

My son is not allowing the blisters to slow him down and is starting to get stronger. It is too soon to tell whether our decision to continue walking through the first weekend for ten consecutive days before our first day of rest in Belorado is realistic. What is becoming apparent is the unmanageable task of keeping seven individuals together for five hundred miles. Our young friend, Daniel, is bursting with energy and is now walking farther ahead. He will complete the Camino much earlier than the rest of us. Pablo had never been to Lourdes and took a train from Pamplona to see it. It gives him a chance to hook up with new faces. Nancy and Loretta walk together and prefer to have their backpacks transported. Father Mike has a good walking pace, and Brad and Cathy are trying to stay with him.

Day of Rest

On the seventh day of the Camino, we do an easy eighteen miles to reach Logroño—a large city of almost 150,000 inhabitants. It is a momentous day as we are one hundred miles from our starting point. Already the distance we have walked is more than most of us had ever done. The physical struggles continue, but with each milestone, our determination and confidence grow. Mentally, we are feeling less like outsiders as the habits of the Camino become engrained in our daily routines. It does not take long for people to begin adjusting to a new environment—especially when the options are limited.

Today, my son and I reclaim our own backpacks! We are both excited in our own way. I was able to lend him a hand and happy to see his progress while getting back my own backpack. He has gotten stronger and is without question ready to carry the heavier load. The blisters persist, but he seems to be dealing with them. His inner strength and positive outlook are not dampened by the size of the peeling skin on both feet. He's never expressed any doubts about reaching Santiago.

Exchanging backpacks for the first one hundred miles was good for both of us. He had time to adjust to hiking while I built up my stamina. The *albergue* here is quite comfortable with cool running water to soak our tired feet under shady trees. Father Mike jokingly suggests that I build a similar apparatus at home. Blisters, bruised bodies, and assorted remedies are sprinkled in conversation. Someone suggests a daily double dose of ibuprofen. The bottom of my feet aches against the rough terrain, and my little toes are pressed tight causing minor discomfort. That is to be expected—a part of the experience. I have no need for medication. Wearing sandals after each day's hike provide adequate relief from the day's battles. As Mijo and I make our walking plans for the following day, the confidence of reaching every destination on our own, so far, is empowering.

Our initial day of rest finally arrives after 150 miles of walking over ten consecutive days. Five of us stay in the same hostel on Saturday evening, a few blocks from downtown. Belorado's population of two thousand is at least quadrupled and bustling with great anticipation for tomorrow's bullfights. A massive stage is seen from all angles of the circular plaza as huge speakers fill the evening air. Mijo and I find it impossible to break through the hordes of revelers to check up on Nancy and Loretta.

It appears I'm beginning to blend in as a bewildered carouser stops me among the crowded plaza to ask directions. The crowds are obviously not all locals with neighboring villagers joining the celebration. The next day, our bodies collapse from exhaustion from ten days of walking without a day of rest. We have been running on empty sustained by adrenalin and grit. Ten days without a break is not wise.

As we leave the beautiful provinces of Navarra and La Rioja, Burgos lies just two days ahead. Navarra is Europe's leader in the use of renewable energy technology, and we see evidence of it everywhere. Rich in its own way, La Rioja's vineyards produce fine wines seen and tasted throughout the Camino. Entering upon the western outskirts of Burgos, we again encounter an exceptionally clean city. The full Camino Frances is a long westward movement with the rising sun on our backs against the coolness of dawn.

Pay Me Later

———— ✑ ————

Before leaving for the Camino, Father Mike and I talk about finding a way to be grateful guests. He settles on picking up trash that fellow pilgrims discard along the way. It is likely not a common scene, and his gesture caught the attention of other pilgrims. Every bit helps. Lacking his spirit and energy, I created personal cards expressing gratitude to our Spanish hosts and included my contact data. The idea was to hand them out when people (hosts or pilgrims) shared plans to visit Southern California.

Giving freely is a way of the Camino. Some gestures are too obvious to miss while others are so subtly wrapped and unexpected that one might overlook them entirely or even misinterpret them. The unanticipated ones are the most fun, even humorous, like my little foray to a candy store. While my son stays back resting his feet after the day's hike, I wander the little town of candy stores and walk into a huge one with the single desire to satisfy my sweet tooth. Sensing my craving, the friendly vendor raises a huge candy that I can have free if I buy two. I decide one is plenty. As he bags my purchase, he reaches under a table for an even bigger bar of soap smiling and extending a buen camino (Spanish wish for a good journey).

"Buenos días," I shout to the young man tending his garden in the early morning as we walk by his property. He responds in kind and adds, "Gusta un tomate?" Would you like a tomato? Walking toward him, he instructs me to put out both hands and tosses me an extra-large red tomato. "Agradecido," I say and sense that its firmness should easily hold until suppertime. This is clearly a tomato meant to be shared with hungry pilgrims.

On a cool late evening, my son receives an unexpected treat. We're in a small village with light traffic. Returning from dinner, we notice a sizeable group of pilgrims sitting in a circle on the quiet street outside our *albergue*. Evidently, they are recounting Camino stories and playing their guitars. I'm a bit tired and make my way inside to rest while Mijo decides to join them. Later, I learn that some of the pilgrims were providing free treatment for sore feet. Sometimes, we just need to show up.

Everything about the walk through the long beautiful park to reach Burgos's famous cathedral was special. The main walking path is parallel to the main boulevard yet buffeted from vehicle traffic by the Arlanzón River and surrounded by large trees. Our destination this morning is the gigantic cathedral where we plan to meet with others in our party.

Walking along the city's boulevard side of the river, a local suggests that we cross over to the shadier park side of the waterway. We planned to hike on the side of the cathedral but are assured that we cannot possibly miss it. Having crossed the river, a lady confirms our destination is five bridges away and then walks ahead showing us with her fingers how many bridges remain each time we cross one. The park sports numerous important historical monuments including a gigantic statue of El Cid on his warhorse and a modern metallic depiction of man's evolution.

Once in Burgos's multispeared cathedral plaza, we look around for a café and spot familiar faces among the midafternoon masses. Father Mike, Cathy, and Brad are sharing lunch with a local priest and a seminarian. A little later, Nancy and Loretta catch up with us. We are still eating when part of the group rushes across the plaza to tour the cathedral before the afternoon closure for siesta.

In the evening, through Father Mike's connections, José Luis and his wife Begoña, whom none of us had ever met, drive all seven of our small group for dinner at their home and to sleepover. The generous home-cooked meal is a timely comfort as is everything about this welcoming family with a large home to raise five children who are now on their own. Where each of us sleeps becomes a concern for them that we don't share. By now, we are experts at finding places to sleep while they seem to be operating out of a habit of assigning beds. But since they do not know us, they keep making suggestions and then second-guessing themselves. I am part of this scene as they walk me through each of the three floors pointing out who sleeps where.

The couple has an evening church engagement, and she pulls me aside to show me how to operate the washing machine before leaving—another cherished luxury of the Camino! The next morning, in the still dark hours, Begoña prepares an abundant breakfast over our feeble protests. When we are ready to leave, our bighearted hosts transport us back to our path on the Camino. We are overwhelmed by their trust and generosity extended to travelers who no longer feel like strangers.

The young man's simple words, "Pay me later," gave great relief to our aching bodies and peace to our anxious minds. The long hike had been exceptionally trying, the kind where every step requires high concentration and must be taken slowly. Arriving late upon the small village for the night, there was no guarantee of room at the *albergue* and not many lodging options. The thought of a long wait in a slow line to check in or, worse, finding the dreaded sign completo (full) weighed heavy on my mind. Just thinking about having to keep looking for an *albergue* sapped what little energy I had left. "Welcome, go rest and pay me later" were the perfect remedy for tired bodies.

A Camino for Everyone

The popular pilgrim's guidebook that everyone seems to carry warns against walking the long dull mesa and even avoiding portions of city routes like the ones in the city of Leon. Mijo and I decided not to be intimidated by the challenges that the author shared. It was in that vein that we enjoyed the introvert's paradise and the extrovert's purgatory mesa experience. The long flat land gave us an opportunity to recuperate from harder hikes and is a good example of walking partners adapting to a situation and to each other. I had looked forward to the solitude of the mesa, and my son, who is more outgoing, had no reservations about trying it. In the end, he said it was one of his favorite regions to walk.

Each morning after daybreak, we give ourselves about an hour of time alone on the trail. It's my favorite time of the day. The air is cool and refreshing as the sun rises to warm us and dispel darkness. Once we no longer need each other's headlamp, either of us walks ahead about fifty yards. At times, we see other hikers along the way but not always. It's still early. Congestion is heaviest during coffee breaks, lunch, or at day's end. The daily practice of walking before dawn makes finding our way in the darkness tricky. On one occasion, a fellow pilgrim insists we go a particular way against our own judgment. In darkness, we follow his suggested route a short distance before realizing the need to double back. Later, we discover that he was misguiding people to shield his wife responding to nature's call. Pointing to us in public yelling, "Those are the guys that got lost this morning" and then blaming his wife was not the Camino spirit that we had come to know.

Before reaching into the backpack for our early morning supply of bananas, peaches, pears, and nectarines or dry apricots and mixed nuts, we feast on blackberries growing along the Camino. By trial and error, we discover the sweetest blackberries in direct sunlight. I'm grateful for the strategic placement wondering if it traces back to when mercados and towns were less prevalent. The fruit we taste is so fresh whether straight from the Camino or the mercado. It never seems to have been stored for long.

Although the Camino attracts almost as many women as men, bathroom breaks are clearly an unequal experience. I often found myself watering tall bushes on the side of the road. An American couple living in Panama told of how they got lost for a day. She happily recounted having two opportunities for bathroom breaks on the deserted road. Almost every town, regardless of size, has well-maintained bathroom facilities. However, lights can suddenly go off, and if you did not bother to scope the location of the switch, it can prolong your stay.

Mijo and I took turns using the facilities, trading off on watching our backpacks and ordering food. Given the masses of hikers, I am really surprised and thankful for the cleanliness throughout the whole Camino. Even small towns sport large recycling bins, and occasionally, we encounter early morning cleaning crews power washing streets and sidewalks. Dining areas often provide small trash receptacles on every table.

Aside from the third day's technology thefts, I am unaware of similar incidents. The only item we lose is a sweatband toward the end of the Camino. That is an amazing testimony given the endless sharing of small space and particularly leaving clothes hanging to dry for hours. To lessen temptation, we maintain close vigilance on our backpacks. During morning breaks and lunch, we prefer sitting outdoors where equipment quickly piles up. We keep ours stacked together and in sight. Our equipment is colorful and marked for easy identification. Keeping track of my son's camera is particularly important as it contains all the pictures along the Camino.

After some time on the Camino, it is easy to spot people on the way to Santiago. They no longer look like tourists. Their walk is different; the clothes are loose, and they seem peacefully in the moment. That image changes dramatically in Sarria—a city only one hundred kilometers from Santiago. Officially, starting the Camino in Sarria warrants a certificate of completion. For those on tight schedules, Sarria is a popular starting point. The newcomers lack the time on the Camino to reorient themselves and tend to be loud and distracting.

Madrid Airport, I'm on the left carrying only a small red backpack.

L to R: Loretta, Brad, Me, Cathy, Father Mike,
Mijo, friend, Nancy, host couple

L to R: Father Mike, Ruben, Cathy, Brad, Nancy, Loretta

Path on the Pyrenees

California Spanish

⚜

Before leaving for the Camino, I receive free advice that my Spanish will be useless in Spain. That is a fallacy. Our California Spanish translated well with few exceptions. We learned that a peach is melocotón, not durazno. Don't ask for a batería; if you need a battery, go with pila. Their tortillas are not flat and thin like ours but rather thick and filled with cheese, ham, and potatoes—a full breakfast in itself. Throughout the Camino, restaurants offer menu de peregrino (pilgrim's menu) for about nine euros. These lunch menus consist of four courses with many choice items. We often tried the vegetable and tuna ensalada mixta—a meat, usually lamb or chicken, or a pasta dish; water and wine are optional, and dessert consists of tres leches, helado (ice cream) or sweet flan. The food is tasty and nourishing, although their thick bread, a kind of bolillo we know in the southwest, is too hard for some tastes.

During morning breaks, I enjoy Spain's café Americano which reminds me of the Starbuck Latte I drink at home. My son's preference for chocolate translates to Cola Cao—a popular Spanish brand. Both drinks are traditionally served smoking hot on small white cups. Served with a fresh Spanish tortilla, you end up with a big, hearty breakfast that will easily tie you over until lunch. We develop a liking for fresh fruit in stands along the Camino, and in super, mercados (markets) are found even in the tiniest villages. Each afternoon, while our clothes are drying, or later in the evening around suppertime, we make our way to the mercado for fruits and nuts for the next day's hike.

Mijo on a cold morning hike

I had expected to translate for my son but found it unnecessary. His Los Angeles experience prepared him well. Within the context of the environment, he picked up specific key words and phrases as needed to express himself. I made it a habit of browsing through the daily newspapers in coffee shops looking for major events and news of the World Basketball Cup taking place in Spain. The only time that language became more difficult was in Galicia where they speak Galician. But even that is a Romance language related to Portuguese and highly recognizable to Spanish speakers.

Perhaps the most fascinating phenomenon about the entire Camino concerning language and communication is the point that language is much more than words. The universal shared experience of pilgrimage transcends cultures, words, and histories that enables people to communicate their wishes without the common need for an agreed upon set of familiar words.

A crucial feature of the Camino that serves as a communication bridge is people's openness to the needs of their fellow pilgrims. When specific terminology is called for, the resources abound to help each other communicate. This was evident in many forms throughout the Camino and certainly regarding basic necessities. Those who sought others to communicate their message usually found a willing hand nearby.

Weather and Bedding

⸎

Where I live in California, the average number of sunny days per year is 278 with average low temperatures of forty-five degrees in January and average high temperatures near ninety in July. I am used to cozy climate.

The weather during the entire Camino was better than we expected. On a few occasions, we got some heavy rain while hiking or had to negotiate mud puddles from the previous night's rainfall. On these taxing instances, our hooded rain jackets serve us well. They are light and long and keep us from freezing. During the hefty downpours, hikers seek shelter in the warm cafes along the way, carefully maneuvering without destroying property. Our choice of rain jackets over ponchos was a good one.

On a cool evening, we get a taste of how torrent rain can suddenly fill the streets and halt pedestrian traffic. We had just gone out for supper and a game of foosball and are only a few blocks from the *albergue* where our jackets are. Suddenly, a powerful storm thunders loudly creating streams of gushing water covering both street and sidewalks within minutes. We looked at each other expecting to remain in the shelter of the restaurant for a long time. We are not on flat land, and as swiftly as the thunderous rain arrived, it disappears.

Albergues have only a few basic commonsense rules to operate efficiently and serve thousands of weary pilgrims each year. Most are not open until the early afternoon to allow time for cleaning after the morning group departs. Handing over one's credencial to the receptionist for the official stamp and paying the lodging fee gets you a bunk but with no guarantee of whether you get a bottom or top one. Some people seem to prefer a bottom bunk, and they fill up first. Once hikers get into the Camino spirit, after a few miles on their feet, they are happy to get any bed. *Albergues* get pretty crowded with all bottom and upper bunks occupied and can house anywhere between forty to two hundred people. The steel framed bunks are made to house a lot of pilgrims with minimal space for movement. We make a point of putting all our gear under our bunk, but that is not the norm.

Shoes are removed immediately upon entering *albergues* and not worn in the sleeping areas. Normally, wooden cabinets or boards are set up outside the sleeping quarters for storage of footwear. Mijo wears extra-large boots which makes them easier to find when we need them before daybreak. I always tie my shoes to his boots and place them at the highest point possible for easy retrieval.

clothes wash basin

Finding an unused sink to wash and a clothesline for drying can be a bit of a cat and mouse thing but a problem solved by waiting. Practicing patience is part of the Camino experience as pilgrims engage in similar tasks around the same time. Sometimes. lines form to take showers or even for toilet use. Occasionally, showers are gender specific but not always. Most offer privacy under tight quarters, but we did experience a few showers without doors.

Albergues close at 9:00 p.m. with all lights out and doors locked. On an engaging evening of cards, we return a bit late and find ourselves locked out. The volunteer Camino host (receptionist) is gone, and all is quiet inside. Desperately peering through the main entrance, eventually, we catch a shadow of someone by the front door who takes pity and let us in.

Our light silk liners prove adequate without a need for a sleeping bag. Scant ventilation, however, is a problem on warm nights, and although we spray for bugs, I was attacked twice with itchy markings lasting a whole week. We find that most pilgrims like to hike early or at least wake up early for breakfast. On most days, we are on the road by 5:30 a.m. with our bright headlamps on until the day's new light breaks through.

Don't Touch the Fruit!

—— ✑ ——

Spaniards are such great hosts that the exception really stands out. We unearthed her at a mercado while looking for fruit. Her tiny store near an *albergue* was a relentless revolving door with pilgrims on the same mission. Upon opening the screen door to her business, an immense pile of ripe bananas greeted customers. Potassium is like gold to hikers, and the natural reaction was to reach for the bananas. Each touch trigged a very loud and lengthy sermon on the virtues of refraining from touching bananas. Each of her reprimands begin with an emphatic, "Don't touch the fruit!" followed by endless motives why clients ought not to touch. Customers were initially startled but rescued when the next client innocently reached for the bananas. Most patrons stepped aside quickly casting baffled eyes at each other while making hurried purchases and rushing out. Evidently, the woman's approach did not hurt her business with one-time buyers.

Along the vastness of the Camino, there are a wide variety of fruit trees and vegetables tempting to the eye and easily accessible to hikers. Some of the large trees from private front yards stretch out unto sidewalks bearing their fruit within reach. In other cases, farmers dispense with building fences to protect their harvest, perhaps trusting or at least hoping that wanderers will respect the sanctity of their private property. By late summer and early fall, when most people show up to walk the Camino, the fruit has reached its ready stage.

On a beautiful brisk and busy morning, about a dozen hikers are walking along a wide dirt road leaving behind a small village that hosted us the previous night. The sounds of people waking up and beginning their day's work and activities are beginning to make their presence. Rich open farmland lie on both sides of the road with intermittent fruit trees exposed between the farms and the road. I catch up with some hikers and happen to be walking between a husband and wife about to reenact the account of Adam and Eve.

She first notices the lavishness of bright red apples hanging from a large tree nearby and strides off the walking path to explore. Having found the tree within easy reach, she starts to gather the biggest apples she can find then rushes back to her husband. All the time, he has been a detached spectator, but now she hands him the fruit to slice which, of course, he dutifully complies. Distracted by their deed, they fail to notice a clandestine man on a motorcycle watching the whole scenario from the side of the road ahead.

When the husband unquestioningly finishes cutting the fruit, he takes a bite and then gleefully starts offering pieces to other walkers around him. Some resist the temptation but many go along. As the group reaches the space where the motorcyclist awaits, he casts his eyes directly on the husband and asks about the apples to which the husband, pointing to his wife, replies, "She gave them to me."

A couple of days later, we are reminded how difficult lessons can be. It is another serene and cool day—perfect for hiking. Mijo and I finally meet up with our pilgrim friend, Pablo, who is back from Lourdes. We have not seen him since landing in Madrid. Evidently, he spent a few days walking with a friend who has moved on. Pablo is now hiking with Bill, his new buddy from Texas. I decide to pass on the benefit of the apple experience, and as I near its conclusion with a warning about resisting temptation, Pablo leaves me hanging in mid-sentence dashing off the road to pick pears.

"Don't touch the fruit!"

Organic Friends

The Camino is truly an organic community of diverse friendships. Martin Sheen's movie *The Way* illustrates this point perfectly. The reasons people are drawn to the Camino from assorted regions of the world are as diverse as their own backgrounds. How well do we really understand the reasons we are drawn to anything? Do our motivations only become clearer with time and especially reflection? Anyone who has been on the Camino or had a similar experience knows how artificial differences melt more easily under shared experiences, especially difficult ones, while similarities are enhanced. It is the heart of team building and making new friends.

People who arrive on the Camino alone have the option of safeguarding that circumstance or exercising the freedom to accompany others. Those whose country of origin is very dissimilar to Spain find security in numbers, although the Camino is not unsafe. Configurations of travelers come in all shapes and sizes. We saw a couple with their preschooler on the Camino, a family with teenagers, a man with prosthetics walking by himself, and quite a few spouses. We ran into plenty of men and women traveling alone and more than one father and daughter pair. Interestingly, we did not see another father and son pair. I wonder why that is. When the subject arose in conversation, some men commented how they would like to do the Camino, or wish they could, with their sons. A man from Australia remarked, "I had four sons. Two died, and I don't think either of the two I have would walk with me."

Finisterre 2014: L to R: Me, Cathy, Brad, Mijo

Pilgrims need quality time to themselves. A typical day on the Camino includes many occasions for interaction with large crowds. The best prospect for time alone is on the trail between meals. Park benches, peaceful spots by the many rivers along the way, or quiet time around church buildings are not hard to find. Many small villages line the Camino and, by their nature, are not noisy or heavily trekked places. Walking alone is a great way to multitask. I find that movement of the body in rural areas seems to activate both my mind and heart the most. It is the setting where resting thoughts awake.

In essence, the Camino experience offers the gift of time to reflect on what we hold dear and to reconnect with our rooted values. What we discover is just how much these crucial aspects of our being have been compromised in our fast-paced competitive world. We all need to spend quality time in settings that allow for peaceful introspection. But it is not the normal condition most of us experience within our family or workplace. We need to create those places and find those spaces. They are necessary in order to catch our breath and ponder our human condition.

Gifts for the Soul

⎯⎯⎯⎯⎯ ✑ ⎯⎯⎯⎯⎯

Camino gifts come in many forms. People have enjoyed the beautiful pictures and videos that my son took on the trails to Santiago and into Finisterre. His cooking skills came in handy in *albergues* with small kitchens for pilgrims' use. On several occasions, we bought the ingredients, and he cooked dinner for large groups. One of the *albergues* had a small refrigerator, and we left wrapped portions of leftovers for the next arrivals. Other pilgrims invited us to share in their meals or exchange portions of each other's treats.

On two separate instances, merchants reverently explain the spiritual significance of their medallion gifts to us, which include miracles and protection on the Camino. One of the storekeepers leaves the counter unattended to bring us our coffee outside on the patio and proceeds to explain the importance of carrying Jesus's mother with us. We are not the only ones sitting outside, and everyone receives a free medallion. We thank him and attach the light medallions to the backpacks reassured that we don't walk alone or defenseless. The little medallions are great reminders of the inherent value of sharing freely from the heart. I came to appreciate them much more than an expensive gift that I don't need. They remain attached to my backpack years after having received them.

The best time to explore easily is after securing lodging for the night and having taken a shower. In the quiet city of Fromista, I stroll along a massive sidewalk lined with evergreen trees and strike up a conversation with a local man on a comfortable bench. Time passes quickly in easy conversation, and Rodolfo asks whether I am interested in anthropology to which I admit, "Well then, why don't you come with me?" he asks in Spanish. Not knowing exactly where he is taking me, I follow him as he turns opposite the sidewalk toward a big building with a sign of his Museo Histórico-Etnográfico de Fromista. He unlocks the gate to his personal treasures and gives me a thorough one-man tour. As I prepare to leave, I see Father Mike, Cathy, and Brad approaching and ask if they would like a tour. I do the introductions, and Rodolfo takes over.

Villadangos Del Paramo is a tiny village with only a couple of stores. After buying snacks for the following day, Mijo and I have time for a game of cards at the only bar in town. The six or so local customers take turns glancing at the television, greeting customers as they arrive, and chatting with the bartender. We settle into a comfortable table by a large window with an idle view of the empty street pulling out the cards for a game of gin rummy. After a while, we notice nothing has changed since we entered the peaceful bar. Time is at a standstill. Except for the television, the whole scene could be from previous generations. Even the people's demeanor is different. They are in the moment. No one is looking at their watch or using cell phones. Whenever any customer gets up to leave, he extends his farewells to everyone including us. We notice too that when anyone walks in, those inside look up to acknowledge the new arrival. We glance at a clock and rush out as the *albergue* closes at 9:00 p.m.!

For its simplicity and vigor, the gift from a woman in Sahagún was perfect. In a scene increasingly familiar on the Camino, we notice pilgrim crowds have taken over the patio of a corner coffee shop on a busy intersection. The outdoor gathering seems cozy under full trees with an expansive view of the busy street. As we arrive, a table empties, and we pounce on it. My son remains outside watching our bags, and I step into a crowded small room to place our order. The sole employee looks up at me with a warm smile and a greeting. She does that every time a customer walks in and starts working on each order immediately. A highly visible customer is fidgeting impatiently for his numerous coffees and getting more irritated every time the waitress looks up to say hello and start a new order. I love her unshakable demeanor in the midst of apparent chaos. I take our drinks and offer a tip which she declines with "I'm only doing my job." She remains undeterred. When everyone finally gathers on the patio, the waitress strides gingerly around packed tables passing out freshly baked cookies.

Most businesses close on Sundays and every day during the midafternoon siestas. Churches in small towns are often locked down except for an hour or two once a week, if they open at all. Medical hospitals and pharmacies seem plentiful, but we find only one hospital for the soul. Two strangers, who became friends on the Camino, used their imagination and personal experiences to create a center for pilgrims to feel welcomed, refreshed, and grounded. Their hospital for the soul is in the middle of town. There is no entry fee, only soft lights, rising smoke from the fresh incense, walls covered with captivating photos of the Camino (lots of shadows), and soothing guitar sounds to heal tired souls.

We wander the long cool room stepping into a narrow corridor in the back where a man is peacefully weaving with his hands. I imagine he is one of the founders of the soul hospital. He appears completely absorbed in his work and no words pass between us. Turning to exit the center, we see a sign that reads, "You don't do the Camino with your feet." That phrase has remained by my side for years. What a helpful and significant observation to look beyond the obvious and find its deeper meaning. Having a sense of purpose (direction) in life is crucial so that we may know if we are on the right path which we navigate with our heart.

The Swap Meet

⟶ ⟪⟫ ⟵

One of my favorite eating spots was not a restaurant but a make-shift rectangular aluminum shelter with long wooden benches on unleveled dirt ground, which we almost missed. Had we followed the practice of meandering off until seeing crowds outside the more popular restaurants or had we been near the town's plaza, we would have entirely overlooked our find. This was our lucky day.

We reached Sarria early Saturday afternoon, and once settled in, I asked one of the locals where she went for lunch. Sizing us accurately by our peregrino garb, she pointed the way and muttered, "La Feria." This sounds a lot like faire to me, and we head in the direction she indicated focusing our attention on restaurant signs with the word, Feria. We end up in the outskirts of town on a quiet and narrow cobble stone street. There is minimal commerce on one side of the road, and on the more sporadic side, which we ignore, are mostly warehouses. We don't see any restaurants.

Something is off kilter. We walk only a few blocks from where we started, and the town feels abandoned, except for a lively swap meet we passed on the opposite side of the street. Could this be one of those restaurants totally quiet on the outside and breaming with activity in the back? We take a futile second look around before doubling back pausing for a quick peek at the swap meet.

The swap meet is packed with locals spread everywhere examining the merchandise and trying to strike deals on their favorites. Our snooping is rewarded when thick white smoke coming from behind the main entrance catches our attention. Two huge grills are turning out fresh octopus, ribs, and steak—La Feria!

For a couple of tired and starving hikers, this is the perfect site! Open air, lots of tasty food, and no hurry to go anywhere. We didn't. Once seated, a friendly waitress walking around the long picnic tables with fresh cheese on a wooden platter cuts us both big slices of goat cheese. The meal includes lavish portions of the grilled helpings, bolillo bread, and a bottle of La Rioja wine. The clientele chatters away freely, and all is good. We have absolutely no commitments after our late lunch, and I am in no hurry to leave.

I drank very little alcohol on the Camino, and my son does not drink at all. Today is the exception, for me. After the meal, I inform Mijo that I am not letting the wine go to waste. Shortly after he leaves, a Canadian couple shows up looking for me. I am the only hiker in the noisy group, and they spot me immediately. I had not met them before, but they had evidently approached Mijo on the street asking for a good place to eat. He told them to look me up at La Feria.

The Long Hike

It is our final week on the Camino, and we are both feeling strong, confident, and healed. We have grown familiar with the ways of the Camino, although its rhythms have been disrupted by the hordes of locals starting their journey in Sarria. From our stay in Palas de Rei (King's Shovels), a short hike puts us in the province of A Coruña where Santiago de Compostela reigns as capital of the Galicia region. The final three legs of the Camino are fourteen, sixteen, and thirteen miles long, and we are ahead of schedule. Our overnight plans in Leon did not materialize due to lack of space in the condo where Father Mike and others stayed, and we decide to bypass the pre-planned Sunday break in Sarria and walk instead.

On Tuesday, September 30, having crossed six river valleys and reached the day's target, Mijo and I are too energized to stop walking. The excitement of arriving soon at our final destination and completing the five-hundred-mile journey kicks in. What the last five weeks have done to our bodies is pretty amazing. Initially, we were relieved to reach our goal for the day's walk and settle in. Now, doing a full stage does not seem enough.

It's been over a week since we last saw some of the members of our party. We don't really know who is ahead or behind us. All we know is that we do not want to stop walking. After doing twenty miles, another burst of energy kicks in; we are reluctant to call it a day. I am aware that other hikers pushed too hard and hurt themselves, and I tell myself that their attempts were too soon into the journey, and they were not ready. Still, I am conscious of my age and need for caution.

As we continue walking deep into siesta time, we encounter fewer hikers and the sporadic businesses in unpopulated areas are closed. Our map shows no lodging options nearby. We are feeling too good to be concerned and assure each other of our good state of being. It is a pleasant late afternoon with overcast skies and great conditions to maintain hiking.

Just on time for a much-needed break, we reach the little village of Oxen with a roadside coffee shop and several large camping tables outside. It is the only source of food that we have seen for a while, and it does not look like anything else is coming up soon. We take the opportunity to stock up on refreshments and inquire about lodging.

It is late; I am tired, and I am hoping the storekeeper takes pity on us and offers a place to stay overnight. When I explain our need for rest and ask his advice, he minces no words, "Well, you can either go back or keep walking." As we rise to resume our journey, a couple of women hikers appear from nowhere and order huge glasses of beer. Either they know something we don't, or they don't care to know.

On the road again, we meet up with a French woman who is lost and in serious need of a bath. She pulls out her maps and asks that we point out our location. We try to help her and also show her the location with our own map that is clearer and more concise. She is not satisfied with our assistance. I let her know that we are heading toward an *albergue* and am not sure how else to help her.

When we finally reach O Pedrouzo, a cool mountainous city only thirteen miles from Santiago, Mijo suggests that we continue to our ending point (thirty miles for today is not enough?). He is not the same person I started walking with a month prior. I had sensed the gradual transformation, and now, thirty pounds lighter sans fresh blisters, rest just gets in the way of a good long hike.

> Give me my scallop shell of quiet,
> My staff of faith to walk upon,
> My scrip of joy, immortal diet,
> My bottle of salvation;
> My gown of glory, hope's true gage;
> And thus I'll take my pilgrimage. (Sir Walter
> Raleigh, 1604)

Santiago

⸻ ❧ ⸻

O ur final leg is a short one, only thirteen miles long. It feels different from all others. We walk with more space between us, content at completing our five-hundred-mile goal but with a tinge of sorrow that the Camino Frances is ending. What has become a normal attentiveness to finding an *albergue* disappears along with sleeping by nine, filling our water container each morning, and a host of other daily routines that had occupied our minds. Are we feeling a physical or mental or spiritual change? If we do not compartmentalize too readily, we might respond, "Yes, we are."

We each lost thirty pounds. I lost half in preparation, and Mijo lost all on the Camino. It was not what we set out to accomplish; we certainly ate no less on the Camino. Losing weight and being physically fit is a component of the Camino. We both feel energized and very capable of walking all day. Getting up early to meet the new day before the crack of dawn is a joyous thing as is eating three hearty meals with minimal healthy snacks between meals.

We both felt challenged by the Camino and greatly rewarded with reaching Santiago. Mijo showed great persistence and determination without the benefit of time to prepare at home. He never wavered on his goal to walk the entire way. It was interesting to see how we each drew on past experiences for confirmation that we were not over our heads. I found myself back at Army Basic Training screaming that it is all, "Too easy, Sergeant"! He drew on his training for a black belt in Taekwondo. Perhaps, it was a case of I've done this before. I know I can.

Commercial signs and city traffic announce our arrival in Santiago. After our arrival, we walk a block from the cathedral and find an outdoor table to relax and watch the faces of pilgrims walking in. Among the happy horde, we spot Pablo and Bill doing their last walk together and call out to them. They are too overjoyed to pause and give us a quick wave.

That afternoon, we wait in a long line to receive our hard-earned Compostela—the official certificate of completion written in Latin and indulgenced since the Middle Ages. Mijo alertly requests both our names on it dated October 1, 2014. This was my Camino and my son's, and over the course of five hundred miles, it becomes our Camino: a father and son's walking experience. It is an exceptionally special time for us. I feel immense gratitude for forty-three days with my adult son. He is a great support in many ways, and I am thankful for sparing me, "I wish my son would join me on the Camino."

The next day, we attend a packed and joyous Pilgrims' Mass held daily in the Cathedral of Santiago de Compostela. We see masses of tourists snapping one more picture on their vacation tour and happy pilgrims sealing the completion of a long and arduous journey. After Mass, the "Hymn to Santiago" is synchronized with the spectacular swinging of the enormous Botafumeiro—the famous thuribles in the cathedral. The burning incense in the huge swaying censers blow out smoke of fragrant prayers. We discover later that some of our seven group members were present. We did not see them.

We rent a car for over a week and head toward the beautiful ocean city of Muxia for an overnight stay. We stroll the city leisurely and stop to feel the cool air and listen to the pounding waves. It seems the right way to transition from the Camino. After a restful morning, we make our way to Finisterre for lunch. This is another historically rich city with connections to the Camino. Walking to the car to leave, Brad and Cathy pull their rental right next to ours, and we take a last picture together. We will not see them or other familiar faces until we meet again in the Madrid Airport.

The economy car is comfortable, but I am not. My son does all the driving, and I keep questioning our speed and double-checking the speedometer. The normal driving speed is too fast for me.

The Camino did a number on me, and I had succumbed to it. Inadvertently, I am resisting returning to where I was five hundred miles prior. When we drive passed pilgrims hiking, I feel pulled to join them.

The Camino provides calm periods of solitude to think, to wrestle with uncertainties, and to simply be in the moment. It is not something I find easy to do at home. Using a sports analogy, the Camino is like halftime. It is an opportunity to reflect on your past performance, on how you've played the game of life. You find yourself asking fundamental questions like, Who am I? What am I called to be? How faithful am I to my true identity? Crucial to the half-time analysis is strategizing to be more effective in the second half—when you return home and continue life's Camino.

A final and important part of our journey was for our small pilgrim group to reassemble after our Camino experience for an evening of thanksgiving. Four months after our initial group gathering for prayer and a farewell blessing, we come together in my home for a post Camino prayer offering and dinner. Bishop Vann and Father Mike lead us again in prayer to culminate and celebrate the Camino.

My son created Camino videos with background music and picture collections. Other pilgrims brought their own pictures or journals and shared their most memorable stories. Mijo videotaped those who walked the Camino as they discussed their impressions and considered incorporating into their homelife the lessons they distilled.

Camino Questions

What should I take with me?

This is a highly personal decision. Some people choose to be in contact with the outside world through social media. Others need medication or elect to carry extra health-related aids in case they need them. Earplugs, books, and journals are popular items. We even saw people carry gloves and "nicer" clothes. Most people do not take a sleeping bag. We found no need for one. The silk liner we took was fine. An extra set of shoelaces came in handy, but the clothesline I took was not necessary. My advice is to travel light. Take care of your body, and do not overburden it with items you "might" need. If you truly need something you left behind, chances are you'll find it in Spain. The one indispensable item to take is an open mind. Be open to whatever comes your way. The Camino is full of surprises. You might as well enjoy them.

What are the showers like?

The good news is that showers are found everywhere. Even the smallest *albergues* have them. Expect tight quarters and little privacy. Actually, showers offer a lot more privacy than my gym but not nearly the space to move about. I attached a small plastic loop on a tiny bag of toiletries that became very useful on doors with hooks. In unexpected places, my son's presence was helpful like when I forgot my soap, and he could lend me his from the adjacent shower. On occasion, we had to wait in line for a shower, but most often, there was little to no wait time. If you stay in a hostel or hotel, accommodations are upgraded. You might try it as a treat and for extra rest. Above all, keeping in mind that you are not on vacation will help you adapt to the Camino.

What is lodging like?

There are plenty of lodgings along the way. Even the smaller towns have some sleeping facilities. Many pilgrims prefer *albergues municipales*, which are city-owned and less expensive. These *albergues* are usually larger and, consequently, more crowded. If you suffer from claustrophobia, the municipals are not for you. Some *albergues* take reservations but not all. Hotels and hostels are often not found in small villages. *Albergues* are furnished with only the basics, and there are not great differences among them. You'll get clean linen including a blanket and pillow. You'll sleep in a bunk that is okay for people under six feet tall. My son, at four inches over six feet, managed to sleep but not terribly comfortable. A few *albergues* are equipped with small kitchens for hikers to use. This is a great way to build community on the Camino. Regardless of your sleeping habits, expect to sleep and awake early.

How is the food?

We often commented about the juicy and sweet taste of the fresh fruit. Peaches, pears, and bananas were among our favorites. All along the Camino, businesses are adept at serving a constant flow of hungry pilgrims, and they are good at what they do. We found the food plentiful, tasty, and inexpensive including lamb, chicken, beef, and fish along with rice, potatoes, and vegetable salads. The service is also very good when you consider that people tend to gather for dining around the same time. Patience is a welcome virtue on the Camino. Many places offer a generous and inexpensive Menú de Peregrino (pilgrim's menu) for about ten euros. Restaurant personnel often speak English.

What are the people like?

Something good happens to pilgrims on the Camino, although it takes time. We all arrive in a hurried condition filled with uncertainties—a state that can help propel us toward fresh insights about ourselves and others or one that can solidify our preconceptions. The Spaniards we met accept pilgrims as a way of life—a source of economic vitality and even as fellow sojourners on the same Camino of life. I love the evening culture centered around the plazas where the adults dress up and congregate while the kids play soccer. The diversity of pilgrims makes the gatherings an international human experience.

How hard is it to do the Camino?

There is not one way to do the Camino. If you intend to walk the whole way, which is my preferred mode, get in shape before you try it. Ideally, you should prepare physically, mentally, and spiritually to prepare well for the Camino. Some people do the Camino by bus or walk only part of the way. Others pedal their way on bike. In Sarria, a hundred kilometers from Santiago, they rent horses to finish the Camino. The best advice is to prepare and not rush through the experience. The Camino is an opportunity to slow down our hectic pace. I walked the entire Camino carrying my own gear at sixty-eight years old. It was challenging, but the preparation at home made it possible for me to do it comfortably.

What is the weather like?

We were in Spain from late August to early October, and the weather was exceptionally good for hiking. We were extremely blessed with excellent walking weather and infrequent showers. We did use our rain jackets on several occasions and particularly in the early morning. When it rained hard, the intensity was more than we normally see in Southern California. Generally speaking, be prepared for rain. Santiago de Compostela has the ominous reputation of averaging over three hundred rainy days per year. Another way to gauge the weather is that we hung our clothes to dry in the early afternoon, and by the same evening, they were almost always completely dry. The wind currents help.

How expensive is it?

If you are walking the Camino, the biggest expense may be the flight. However, if you decide to stay in hotels or hostels, costs will increase. If you plan any time away from the Camino, consider meal and hotel costs, which are comparable to the US or even higher. You can keep costs down by walking and staying in *albergues* for seven to ten euros a night and dining on special meals for hikers, "Menú de Peregrino," which are bountiful and healthy meals. The cost of an *albergue* is the same as a meal or even less.

What can I expect from walking the Camino?

It's a good idea to think about what you hope to get from the Camino experience and, as important, what you plan to give. For those who lead exceedingly busy lives, the time to exercise and catch your breath may be enough. For me, spending over forty days with my adult son was a very special time that I never thought I'd experience. Going on your own is very doable, but having someone with you that you can count on is a bonus. We had no problem making the necessary adjustments to companion each other.

Is water hard to find?

No. Drinkable water is abundant and easily accessible along the Camino in most towns and cities. Many locales place centrally located fresh running water for the townspeople and pilgrims to use. Water is scarce where villages are far apart. We each carried a three-liter water container (a CamelBak) and filled it at every opportunity. At the end of each day, we cleaned it and again filled it completely in the morning before setting out. We took a sixteen ounce bottle for daily doses of electrolyte powder mixed with water.

How much money should I take with me?

There is no need to carry much money. Spain and France accept most major credit cards, but you don't want to carry more than one. We established a special account for the Camino and carried only a debit card. We found ATMs in the larger cities. My son and I both slept with our passports, debit card, and paper currency in our pants' pockets. If you intend to see more of Spain after the Camino, count on extra costs. We rented a car and, after a week of driving around, dropped it off at the Madrid International Airport. Consider some quiet time for reflection after the Camino. If you can do that while in Spain, it may be easier than at home.

Is it safe to travel alone?

I went with my son and five other friends and found it hard to keep together as each settles into a personal pace. However, my son and I committed to staying together and that worked out great. We were alone only when we chose to be which became a daily habit during the early part of each day. We met a significant number of people who arrived on the Camino unaccompanied but, in reality, were not alone as they befriended others and joined groups of travelers. The Camino is quite safe. I was amazed at how many women went alone without speaking Spanish or English, which are the more prevalent languages.

What if I get hurt?

It is not unusual to suffer some injury on the Camino; after all, you are walking five hundred miles. Many pilgrims take some form of first aid including moleskin and ibuprofen. Keep in mind that Spain is interested in creating a welcoming and supportive setting for hikers and pharmacies are plentiful. We saw many signs announcing the locations of hospitals for people with more severe needs. Taking the proper hiking equipment and preparing physically are essential first steps in avoiding serious injury.

What are the trails like?

I suppose the best way to answer this question is not very specifically as you pretty much encounter every type of trail. In wet conditions, everything changes and can be a real challenge for those of us who wear glasses. I had not realized how much walking is on hard surface, but it is significant. I got my first glimpse of this phenomenon on the initial day's walk over the Pyrenees where about half the trail is paved. My greatest challenges were the rocky steep descents when wet. These require a great deal of concentration and are acutely difficult on the feet. The lonely mesa, which has a bad reputation for its unattractiveness, was actually a relaxing place for me to walk on level ground.

Where is the best place to start the Camino?

The Camino is not one single path but many, like spokes on a wheel with Santiago in the center. My son and I did the popular French Camino which starts on the French side of the Pyrenees in Basque Country. The only reason to start in Spain is if you have serious concerns about your physical condition, but then, why would you be walking the Camino? I wholeheartedly recommend not skipping the French part of the Camino. Start in Saint-Jean-Pied-de-Port. That first leg is a relatively difficult climb, but the scenery is exceptionally inspiring and unmatched anywhere else on the Camino.

Did you encounter any surprises?

I am happy to say that the surprises I encountered were not problematic, with the exception of the bathroom lights that turn off by themselves in many of the bathrooms throughout the Camino. We saw some huge dogs the size of small ponies. The weather was much better than I expected. My two biggest and most welcome surprises were that my hikes at home were more demanding than those on the Camino and seeing my son's transformation from beginning to end. He had little time to hike at home and break in his equipment. By the end, he didn't want to stop walking.

Carrying his heavier backpack during the first week, while he adjusted to the Camino, made me vulnerable as did the failing of a hearing aid. Combined, the two events helped ground me in the ways of the Camino. The Camino grants blisters, falls, and injuries indiscriminately. Individuals exercise their own response-ability. My son assured me on day one that he would prevail and finish strong. He did.

How do you end the Camino?

Along with hundreds of weary and appreciative people from all over the globe, we attended the special pilgrim Mass in Santiago de Compostela. I am sure not all in attendance are Catholic, and it matters not. We are all fellow pilgrims on the Camino, and church does not seem like the place to part ways. After walking five hundred miles, we learn that the Camino is life. It continues. We do our best to cooperate with it and realize that, ultimately, it shapes us. And yes, we do not do the Camino with our feet.

The North Camino

Four Years Later

———— ⌘ ————

There is no way to walk the entire Camino and not feel in awe of its beauty and serenity and, if you open your mind to it, a mysterious magnetic pull. The Camino coalesces time with natural splendor, profound history, and a blending of people from all continents. Every day is truly a new experience filled with hope, trust, and boundless possibility. I have never felt more whole and fulfilled than on the Camino. Explaining the Camino experience is not easy and not returning to do it again is hard.

A couple of years after walking the Camino, I started feeling a growing desire to revisit it but felt it important not to return too soon. I wanted ample time to process and live the initial experience more fully. One way to do that was to continue hiking regularly at home. Four years later, the right time had arrived.

I love the French Camino, and my initial plan was to walk it again. It is so vast and diverse that I knew I would experience it differently the second time. I have friends who did the Portuguese Camino separately (including Brad and Cathy), and they all compared it unfavorably to their French Camino experience. I also thought that I may have to do the Camino alone this time and hoped that my son could get away for a couple of weeks. To my surprise, he was very interested in the entire Camino and could commit six full weeks to it.

As I thought of returning, I noticed my attitude about the Camino evolving differently from the initial excitement of the unknown. I began thinking that walking five hundred miles was not a great challenge. Familiarity with the Camino eliminated prior apprehensions and provoked uncomfortable awareness. Knowing exactly

what to take with me, what to expect for lodging, food, and numerous other prior uncertainties started to create feelings of self-deter-
mination. I was bothered by how easily I was falling into a trap that
could destroy an authentic Camino experience: one still capable of
surprising and baffling the soul. The French Camino had taught me
that you do not do the Camino, the Camino does you. Four years
later, the lesson was unraveling. My self-assuredness was becoming
an impediment to growth, and it seemed I could not prevent it from
creeping in.

Over a casual conversation with an acquaintance, I mentioned
going on the Camino. When I saw him again, a month later, he gave
me a book about a man walking the Camino to help him deal with
his brother's suicide. I had no interest in the topic and did not expect
much from reading the book, if and when I got around to it. After
laying it aside for a while, I finally prodded myself to start reading
and, totally unexpected, unearthed a solution to my rising Camino
concerns. Initially focused on the author's purpose for pilgrimage, I
had not realized that he was not on the French Camino but on the
North Camino, also known as the original or coastal Camino. The
timely discovery (I was just about to make flight reservations for the
French Camino) felt like what I had come to view as a Camino experience: what you need shows up just as you need it.

Reading about the intriguing Camino Norte with its mountain
peaks (Picos Europeos), beautiful beaches, and Basque, Celtic, and
Castilian cultures invigorated me. The Norte is a slightly longer and
more difficult Camino than the Frances. That made me feel better. It
is also cooler and wetter. I was thrilled that it is not nearly as crowded,
which is a growing criticism of the Frances as increasing numbers of
people compete for resources. The book generated a variety of fresh
questions about this Camino, and I became motivated anew by its
possibilities. Swiftly, the nagging feelings of overconfidence began to
disappear. My son is adaptable and a good sport about going along
and agrees we should try the Norte.

Our plan was to start in mid-September. We both prefer cooler
weather and, as an added bonus, by then, the Camino is void of
students and their parents. The first Camino had highlighted the

importance of adequate rest, and we decide to take every Sunday off including the first one after only three days of hiking. Allowing extra time for the unforeseen is important especially if your goal is to walk the entire way to Santiago. Our hope was to have time after the Camino to explore other parts of Spain by car and be home the end of October.

Before starting the pilgrimage, I would complete a ten-month retreat on the Saint Ignatius Spiritual Exercises. My spiritual director, Father Eddie Samaniego, suggested a means of using scripture daily on the Camino. I made all the necessary copies of readings to take with me. My journaling habits had strengthened since the Frances, and I decided to take a small, hardcover journal. I intended to make time for daily contemplation and hoped to write as often.

A Different Mindset

———— ✎ ————

As the idea of journeying a different path germinated, I became increasingly excited. Four years between Caminos meant that I was not exactly in the same place, not entirely the same person. I would be walking a more difficult Camino at seventy-two years. In my preparation and planning, I wanted to be mindful of the changes in me and also make good use of the lessons from the initial pilgrimage. Quite naturally, I started to think about the Camino as a retreat. I had experienced fruitful weekend retreats, and the thought of taking thirty plus days to contemplate in the mountains and oceans of Spain fascinated me.

While the previous Camino melted away many of the rookie questions, a week before departing on the Norte, I wrote in my journal, "Am I adequately prepared?" "Will it rain a lot?" "Is this Camino a good choice?" While I thought that I could walk the Norte, I started to feel that it was not entirely up to me. I would do my part to prepare as best I could and then trust in what developed. This was clearly a different attitude for me. Months before departure, I created an acronym to guide my thoughts and actions. MAP consisted of mindful, attentive, and present, and I assigned a particular meaning to each word. I was to be mindful of welcoming the Holy Spirit each day. Being attentive makes me aware of the visible as well as the invisible of what exists and what once was. To be present helps me to be respectful of what is in front of me at the moment.

The first Camino taught me three things about Spaniards that I wanted to carry with me. The first is their devotion to family as expressed in their daily gatherings in the plazas, dinner conversation, and the inclusion of children and the elderly. Second is their welcoming attitude toward pilgrims. I never hesitated to ask for help and most often received much more than I expected. Pausing for lunch in the middle of a hike, I wanted to spare staff and other diners by eating outside, but they wouldn't have it. Last is their propensity toward cleanliness. This trait is clearly evident throughout the country. The only two exceptions I saw on the French Camino were the mess pilgrims leave on the path and the careless discard of cigarette smokers. The three observations about my hosts coupled with a desire to be mindful, attentive, and present led me to embrace an attitude of gratitude. I wanted to stand with my hosts and show that I believe in their priorities and respect their ideals. To that end, I would carry the Pilgrim Beatitudes to reflect upon while on the Camino.

The Beatitudes of the Pilgrim

1. Blessed are you, pilgrim, if you discover that the Camino opens your eyes to what is not seen.
2. Blessed are you, pilgrim, if what concerns you most is not to arrive, as to arrive with others.
3. Blessed are you, pilgrim, when you contemplate the Camino and discover it is full of names and dawns.
4. Blessed are you, pilgrim, because you have discovered that the authentic Camino begins when it is completed.
5. Blessed are you, pilgrim, if your knapsack is empty of things and your heart does not know there to hang up so many feelings and emotions.
6. Blessed are you, pilgrim, if you discover that one step back to help another is more valuable than a hundred forward without seeing what is at your side.

7. Blessed are you, pilgrim, when you don't have words to give thanks for everything that surprises you at every twist and turn of the way.

8. Blessed are you, pilgrim, if on the way, you meet yourself and gift yourself with time, without rushing, so as not to disregard the image in your heart.

9. Blessed are you, pilgrim, if you search for the truth and make of the Camino a life, and of your life a "way," in search of the one who is the Way, the Truth and the Life.

This time, my physical preparation at home is not nearly as intense. I am using the same backpack, a wider shoe that is a half-size longer, and continue to carry a three-liter water bag. I do not start hiking regularly until five weeks before departure. I hike three or four times weekly, at first on flat surfaces doing six to eight miles. By the third week, I am doing ten-plus miles on steep mountain paths with a full backpack. It is highly unlikely to be able to walk a five-hundred-mile Camino injury-free without training in similar Camino conditions. People without the time necessary to prepare adequately are more likely to end up getting hurt. It should not be a surprising outcome. For someone with sufficient time for conditioning, the main task is to develop a suitable plan and implement it.

During my preparation, I integrate a spiritual dimension. I carry scripture with me (Sunday readings) and devote a day of contemplation to each of four readings. Once I finish the four readings, I spend the remaining three days in review as taught in the St. Ignatian Exercises. The process helps me to connect scripture to my own life as it is today and to everything and everyone around me. It is never a study of what took place a long time ago in a faraway place. The formula that my spiritual director recommends works well for me.

Whatever activity I hope to do on the Camino, I start doing it at home and that includes journaling. Every pocket and space in my backpack are accounted for. I put each item in its strategic place to avoid back injury by using the correct muscles for hauling weight. I fold clothes to make optimal use of space and place items where they will not rattle or move around. What I use most is easily accessible which means I can grab my journal throughout the day, without having to search for it.

When I stop to catch my breath during hikes, I take out my little journal from its designated place in the backpack. For some amazing reason, walking (especially in nature) is the key that opens my heart and mind to the inner world which I believe is fundamental to truly understanding and finding one's true place in the outer realm. The breaks between hikes are optimal times to journal as there is no shortage of material. If nothing else, I write about what I pick up with my senses and the reactions they engender. As a male who falls easily in the trap of living in my mind, I make an extra effort to engage the heart when writing. I find the help I need in this area by carrying with me inspirational little books where I can read just a page or a poem. One of my favorite books that I bought in my thirties is *The Desert Is Fertile* by Helder Camara.

The new balance of less physical preparation and greater spiritual emphasis is different from my first Camino and feels right. I still hope for an "authentic" Camino experience where I can walk the entire way, stay in modest accommodations, and pull my own weight. Yet I am increasingly conscious of the need to be open and accept whatever happens on the Camino. At the time of preparation, I had no idea how much I'd be tested.

Before departure, I need to wrap up and tidy up loose ends around the house and within me. I cut my hair extremely short, one less distraction to fuss with. I decide not to take a razor and allow the beard to sprout. I go to confession as a way of readying myself more fully to accept the Camino on its terms. I visit relatives in the cemetery to discern their wisdom and have lunch with my sisters and other family members. It is all part of the process of surrendering my own agenda, which is what defines pilgrimage.

Finally, my wife, son, and I host a Camino potluck and prayer service as we had done four years prior. We invite friends who had done the Camino and those about to make their first one or doing a return trip. Bishop Kevin Vann leads the prayer service along with Father Mike Hanifin, who is about to accompany a small group of men on their initial French Camino. People bring their backpacks which we line up in the entryway to the house for the Bishop to bless. The array of backpacks fittingly displays pilgrim scallop shells symbolizing the Camino experience.

A few days before my son and I depart, I learn that some of Father Mike's party were not allowed to carry their hiking poles on the plane and were told to bag them and check them in. Luckily, I still have time to order small canvas bags for our collapsible treks. The small gesture saved us time and effort as our poles cleared every security checkpoint without further scrutiny.

On the flight from Los Angeles to London (short layover), I pull out my journal and discover a reassuring note from my ten-year-old godson, John Paul. Among other things, he assures me not to worry about my chickens or my wife. In my absence, he promises to take care of both. What great support! In the meantime, Mijo goes online and makes train reservations from Barcelona to Irun, our starting point.

After a few hours of sleep in Barcelona, we take the early train to San Sebastian with a transfer to the French-Spanish border town of Irun. It is my son's birthday. Within four years, he and I get to spend September 12 in Spain twice. The six-hour train ride is a good way to commemorate the day and see the country from another angle. We have time to acclimate comfortably in a spacious train offering food and drinks. At sixty-five euros each, the train is a good option to flying to San Sebastian. Today's reading, "I will walk before the Lord in the land of the living" (Psalm 116:1–9). I'm ready!

Journal entry

I'm beginning to feel peaceful in this amiable and restful envi-ronment—God's country. The train is so clean as was the hotel and streets in and around the train station. I love Spain!

We reach Irun in the afternoon with a short walk from the train drop-off to the pilgrim two-story *albergue* where we stay with twenty men and four women from several countries. The excitement of the group to start the first day of walking is palpable. Rather than charging a flat fee, the *albergue* accepts donations, not an unusual practice on the Camino. The host is well-prepared to receive pilgrims and offers free hiking gear including water containers, hats, sun lotion, and assorted walking poles. He hands each person a free *credencial* and stamps it. Getting the *credencial* stamped is a pilgrim's daily task to show the route taken and to receive the official Compostela as proof of doing the Camino. The host motions toward city workers outside and tells us there is no hot water for showers tonight. The Camino begins.

There are several restaurants nearby, and we share supper with other pilgrims including Paul from Nevada City and Charles of Canada. Paul wants to practice his limited Spanish and is determined to use only the most proper manner of communication. Sensing that six weeks on the Camino is not going to support his ambitious goal, I encourage him to communicate the best he can explaining that Spaniards will recognize and appreciate his effort, but Paul won't hear of it. If he is unsure of the nuances of a word or phrase, he vows not to use them. It's all Greek to Charles.

Mijo and I awake before dawn the next day. We are the first to leave quietly trying not to disturb those still asleep. From experience, we set about to map out an approach to the Norte. We intend to walk before daybreak while the air is cool, and the body is rested. After a couple of hours, we stop for a hearty breakfast and continue walking until noon to reenergize with a Menú de Peregrino, being careful to eat before siesta time. Afterward, we continue walking another couple of hours and find an *albergue* for the night. We shower, wash our clothes, have dinner, and sleep well. That is the way it is supposed to work. We are about to be introduced to what the Camino has in store for us.

The initial stage is a fairly long and difficult eighteen-mile walk. The prior night, my son and I had scouted the route so that we would find it while still dark. We are excited to begin walking in beautiful, sunny Spain. We start off in drizzling darkness, walking on rocky, steep terrain that is soaking wet with huge puddles. Cautiously and slowly, we trek under large pine trees along the Bidasoa River between Spain and France. I don't mind difficult hikes, but wet rocks are no way to start the Camino! My mind is totally focused on the task at hand, and my eyes are glued to every step I take. The first day on the Camino can be treacherous.

If it were raining hard, we would be unable to walk in darkness. The trickle, however, is constant. Each time I sense it let up; it picks up again. We are forced to pull out our backpack covers and rain jackets. A plastic zip lock bag protects our passports and paper currency. For further protection from moisture, we pull the documents from our pants' pocket and place the plastic bag inside the rainproof jacket. We've been careful to carry only items that are absolutely necessary, and passports top the list. We each carry a picture of each other's passport, and my wife has a copy at home as well.

I am sure the sun will rise soon to warm us and dry out the soggy ground. When day breaks, however, we realize there is no chance of the sun shining through the gigantic thick branches above us, and we can see that the rocky path is the only break in the thick forest. All is not completely lost as we can now see that the enormous boulders on our path are everywhere. We must be smart about maintaining a measured pace and planting our feet solidly every step before attempting the next one.

While training at home, I tried to develop good hiking habits. Eventually, the patterns become second nature, and I use them automatically like driving on cruise control. One of my established routines is to use water liberally. I learn not to wait until thirst sets in. The last thing I need is to dehydrate my body, and I'm convinced that drinking water generously prevents blisters from developing. On our first lengthy, wet hike, I am drinking freely out of my large container. We do not hike far before suddenly realizing that I'm completely out of water! I'm stunned. Never have I not had drinking water on me, and I'm not in a good place to run out. I check for leaks trying to figure out how I ran out so quickly. Luckily, my son, who drinks less than I, still has some, but for how long?

Evidently, the slow pace, short distance covered, and lack of sun threw me into thinking that we had not been walking very long. Backtracking miles for water makes little sense, and we are uncertain how far ahead we can find water. In this ambivalent state of mind, we are elated to see two local men with a dog walking toward us. I don't know where they come from as we cannot see any homes nearby. They tell us of a water well off the main path behind us in the direction they are taking. It's clearly our best option as we need to have water. We follow them and uncover the great pearl of cool, clear water. It is just far enough from the walking path that we would have never found it on our own. I could not thank them enough telling them that they had saved us.

By 2:00 p.m., we finally find a place for a late lunch. We're hungry from all the walking without a full meal. Welcome to the Camino Norte, I tell myself. It is not going to be predictable. Lunch hits the spot, but once we resume walking, my stomach does not feel right and keeps getting worse. It is an unusual condition for someone who rarely gets sick. I was trying so hard to watch every step and avoid injury never suspecting that I could be incapacitated in another way. I don't know whether the culprit is the well water or the food. Mijo consumed the same and feels fine. I keep walking and hoping my condition does not deteriorate.

The Norte has a lot of open space, and the lack of masses of people is a welcome feature. But facilities are predictably less available. That is not to say that they are lacking, only that one must be more vigilant about their accessibility. That was not a huge issue when it came to crossing rivers. The Norte has several sites where you pay a small fee for a ferry to take you across. On the very first hike, we pay a fraction of a euro each for a few minutes on a fairly empty ferry. Evidently, they make several runs each hour during the daytime. We never had to wait for a ferry to show.

Our hike continues in a beautiful, lush, and very wet forest. We are trying to adjust to the terrain and weather while also attempting to find a walking pace that works for both of us. It's been four years since we walked together, and it takes time to match our stride and find our rhythm. Just as important is adapting to each other's tendencies for taking breaks and exploring. My stomach continues acting up horribly. Without a pharmacy in sight, I'm forced to break off the main path.

Unaware of my whereabouts, my son passes me. He finds a cozy private home nearby that welcomes pilgrims for the night providing us with food, shelter, and badly needed showers. A young Jewish family owns the home and uses it to support pilgrims on their journey to Santiago. They don't charge a fee for their service but accept donations. In their front yard sits an enormous tree loaded with ripe figs. In my mind, I picture my year-old aspiring fig tree by my chicken coop as a mustard seed that will spread as large as the one in front of me.

As we settle in, I head straight for the shower as my son washes our hiking clothes and puts them out to dry. He launders by hand as there is no washing machine available to us. The clothesline is by a large picnic table next to another fruit tree. Gazing at the sky, I notice dark clouds settling in and wonder if our clothes will have a chance to dry. We make sure to secure them tightly so they at least remain off the ground. I am so grateful for Mijo's attitude, taking things in stride, and adapting to the circumstance. My journal entry the first day reads, "An eventful day and difficult hike."

Our gracious hosts offer rich, nourishing meals and conversation. They tell us of other similar Jewish communities including one in San Diego, our previous home city. In the morning, my son and I are invited to see their old-fashioned brick furnace where they make their own daily bread. The smell of fresh bread and warm heat radiating from the ample furnace make it tempting to prolong our stay.

Journal entry

At many points today, we walk without seeing another pilgrim on the Camino. It is nothing like the French Camino. The guidebook does a poor job of providing distance information between *albergues* or food sources.

On our second hike, my son receives a text that a fellow employee passed away. During the forty-two days in Spain, we hear a number of significant news about family and friends. This was the first followed by several positive messages. The last one, however, is of my mother-in-law's passing. She was laid to rest at ninety-three years of age, the day after we got home.

Our first break of the day is on a relaxing city bench facing the popular San Sebastian beach, Playa de La Concha. The flawless beach is a stunning, shell-shaped marvel. Even on this cool morning, people are out walking and shopping while others scurry to stake their beach turf. It is a beautiful sight and a very popular summer target. It saddens me to leave this gorgeous place so quickly not knowing if I will ever come this way again. Just outside the city, we see a sign announcing that we are 795 kilometers from Santiago (494 miles). The sign is in Spanish and Euskara.

For the entire first week, we walk in historic Basque Country. Their mysterious language is unrelated to any other known living language. Often, signs are posted bilingually but not always. I can decipher anything in English or Spanish and some French, but nothing helps me unravel the Basque words we encounter. This is not to say that we cannot order food or make sleeping arrangements. The basic needs are handled easily as most local merchants are multilingual, and the *albergue* hosts are usually experienced Camino pilgrims from different nations. Communicating essential needs and accessing services is not an issue on the Camino.

Today, we meet a couple from Australia who walked the French Camino before attempting this one. He is a proficient hiker and carries a light tent which they use this evening. The local Catholic church lets them take a shower and pitch their tent in their property for two euros. We fall short of reaching our day's destination. By the time we find lodging, we settle for a $40 pension (think small inn) with a sparse room and twin beds. The arrangement works well for my son who snores loudly and is unable to rest well. For my part, once my hearing aids are removed, I'm in deep silence.

The contrast to our second night on the Camino four years prior is telling. Having crossed the Pyrenees into Spain, we run into crowds of pilgrims everywhere scurrying to claim a bunk in a 120-bed *albergue*. Nearby, the cafés are abuzz with hungry walkers. Tonight, we are in Orio—a small quiet village. Throughout the day, pilgrims are scarce. The few we encounter seem to reach out more readily than what we saw in the French Camino. Volume always dictates how people interact with each other. When we lived in a small town, people would wave and greet each other from their front yards or while walking or driving. I don't see much of that in Los Angeles.

Journal entry

Today was another tough hike with sharp climbs and descends on rocky paths—especially at the end. We did not hike the distance we mapped out for the second consecutive hike. Arrived too late in Orio to claim a bed, both small *albergues* were full.

When we start walking the next morning, we no longer need headlamps. The journey continues with the warmth of the early sun on our backs as we head west—unlike those driven east of Eden. Coming home is a westward labor characterized by lightening one's load and surrendering the ego; neither is easy even on the Camino. I find that my mantra (MAP) and daily contemplation are best served with an attitude of gratitude for all that occurs to us.

My immediate challenge is eating on time. My diabetic condition is new, and the first thing I learn is to monitor my diet. If the essential food is not available when I need it, then I must carry something substantial with me. Finding the required nourishment on time compels me to walk at a zestier pace, which is the way I prefer to walk. Without reliable information on where we can find food, it makes for an interesting journey.

The first week, we face a particularly steep path leading into the beach city of Deba. We are aware of a long gap between facilities, and our host *albergue* prepares a wholesome sack lunch to take with us. We make sure to get an early start using our headlamps and quickly find ourselves on a spiraling paved road in a forest of thick tall trees. The uninterrupted, lone path gives me the confidence that I can walk briskly without any risk of getting lost or losing sight of my son.

As the path progressively ascends, the air gets lighter and cooler, and soon, a heavy morning fog sets in around me. I can see a hundred yards below, but no one is in sight. Occasionally, I hear the sound of distant barking rising toward me. I am inspired by God's beauty and unperturbed by the demanding climb as I start to sweat profusely. The combination of cold air and warm face cause my glasses to fog up. The smell of fresh trees around, below, and above me is sweet. On the side of the road, I find a set of large, smooth, boulders—a perfect resting spot.

Looking down the winding path between trees, from where I sit, I briefly spot my son and whistle to him. He recognizes the intrusive sound and waves back. It will be a while before he gets here. I make myself comfortable and take deep breaths while wiping my face and glasses. I pull out my water container and begin to relax. My hand instinctively reaches for the journal and pen, but I pull it back and resist writing to quiet myself and savor the moment. It seems the right place to remove my shirt and allow the cool breeze to engulf me. My whole being is at peace. It is a flawless Camino Norte experience: peaceful, natural, and infinite. The picturesque scene is etched it in my mind.

The long hike does not get easier, and we make slow progress. By nightfall, we find ourselves walking on wet rocks without any sign of nearing the next town. I am beginning to give up on finding an open diner and not feeling optimistic about a place to spend the night. Walking in thick woods, we find that ranchers close their heavy wooden gates at night to keep their cattle from wandering. They post signs reminding late pilgrims to close the gates behind us. On this night, we close several gates.

After an exhausting day, we finally reach the city of Deba close to midnight and are lucky to find a café that is already closing. We are mercifully allowed entrance, and the cook proposes to prepare the same meal for both of us. Gratitude at this moment flows easily, and our minds turn to finding a place to sleep since the only *albergue* we found is full. We share our predicament with the waiter, but he is unable to suggest other sleeping options.

Staff needs to close up, and we hurry through our late supper not thrilled about abandoning the warmth of being indoors with no prospects of finding a place to sleep. We thank our meal hosts for their generosity and zipper up our rain jackets to face the cold night. Our alternatives for getting any rest are dreadfully bleak. We walk by a couple of venues with loud music and crowds of young revelers. Spain still has a lot of smokers, and they are here tonight. Desperate for rest, we spot a city park nearby as our best alternative. Without a tent, we settle for a metal bench and decide to take turns trying to sleep as the wind begins to pick up. Dawn will break soon, and we need to be here only a few hours is my mute consolation.

After two Caminos, we have seen help appear unexpectedly when most needed. Mijo calls these episodes "coincidences." It comes now in the form of a dark shadow moving toward us in the pitch black of a cold night. Our waiter of a short while ago finds us and invites us to follow him. We reluctantly agree uncertain as to where he is taking us but thinking it has to be an improvement. In the still of the night, we approach an eerily quiet *albergue* (the full one) with a no vacancy sign, and he unlocks the door. "The bunks are all taken" he says as he tosses a mattress and blankets our way. His kindness fills us with warmth and rest.

Journal entry

Today is a highly memorable day. I love the spiraling, sharp climb in the forest and resting on a huge boulder on top alone. The morning was so peaceful and nature-filled, unlike walking hungry on wet rocks late night with only a piercing light to guide us. We find an isolated pension in darkness and a guest lets us in. Rooms are full, and there is no staff. We continue walking. At the end, we are rescued from sleeping in a park by a humane waiter who sought out two strangers and gave us shelter.

The morning chill affirms that restful sleep on a park bench would have been impossible. We are among the first to awake as our mattress lies by the main entrance. Around us, early risers scuttle around putting on their equipment in whispers trying not to disturb any lingering dawdlers. Oddly, a lady lays a pair of boots by my son and walks away. After a while, a man, who evidently has been frantically searching, asks in broken English if we have seen his boots, and my son hands him the pair beside him noting that a woman lay them there. He takes them abruptly and leaves. Soon after, pilgrims we have not met warn us about a big man stealing shoes. The mix-up is well travelled. Days later, as I relax on a long stretch of road along the beach, the Austrian man who thinks my son took his shoes approaches. We greet each other, and he asks me to take his picture. Afterward, I explain the shoe incident slowly, sprinkling questions to see that he gets it. It seems like he is settled with misinformation and not interested in facts.

The Basque portion of the Norte alternates between ocean and mountain hiking. Sometimes, we do both on the same day. On one such case, we meet up with the only Asian people we see on the Norte—a man and his wife from South Korea. Like others we meet, they too are happy to have walked the French Camino first to prepare them for this one. It seems people like the contrast between two great experiences and doing the easier one first. Looking down from the top of the hill to where land and sea come together is an exhilarating encounter. As we slowly ascend a treacherous narrow path, full of brush and rocks, the view of the vast Atlantic straight down is breath-taking. The concentration required on this hike creates a silence broken only to see how the other is doing. We check in with each other and with our Korean friends. What was posted as a hundred-meter climb turns out to be much longer.

Finally, safe on solid ground, we break at a beach cove and bring out the fruit snacks we've been carrying for a time like this. Our friends invite us for a group picture, and afterward, my son and I remove our hiking shoes and rest our aching feet. Beach strollers are spread along the shore enjoying the warmth of the mild sunshine. Suddenly, our adventurous Irish friend whom we had just met shows up. Vince is on the Camino by himself for two weeks. He seems to make up his itinerary as he moves along. Having lived in various countries, he speaks several languages and seems to adjust easily. After a while, the Asian couple decides to continue walking on the Camino path to find a place for lunch. There is no way that I am not walking along the beach, and I head out in full hiking gear. My little toes have been aching, and I'm counting on the salt water for relief. After a while, I turn around and see Vince following at a distance playing with the tides. My son is farther back, and I don't quite make him out. A rock formation on the beach is a convenient place to wait for him while soaking my feet.

The ocean is a feature of the Norte that even those of us who don't spend much time on the beach can appreciate. There is no better pleasure on the Norte than taking off your hard shoes and dipping your tired feet in salty water. After navigating sharp rocky paths and being treated to unique panoramic views of boundless water, your senses feel full. It is hard to ask for more. But when you reach the beach and remove your shoes, liberating your tired feet takes you to another level. The Camino seems to possess a mystic energy observed through the feet and into the deepest recesses of the mind. It sharpens the senses making them more sensitive and in tune with the environment.

Journal entry

The weather is cool but comfortable. No rain in sight. We had lomo (tenderloin), fries, and a soda for lunch. At $25 a plate, the Norte is more expensive than I expected. I'm so glad this Camino does not have any of the litter seen on the Frances.

The bicyclists, prevalent on the Frances, are hardly seen here. The most unusual means of travel we encounter is a Russian man carrying his old, shaggy dog on a wooden cart resembling a wheelbarrow. When we first meet him, he is gazing at strangers at the bottom of a very long set of stairs waiting for help to carry the cart and dog to the top. We arrive to help him at the same time as a Spanish pilgrim. Sporting a long shaggy beard and weather skin, it is clear that the man has been on the road a long time. At this point, he has traveled over 1,200 miles with his loyal friend.

My son is a trooper. He makes every effort to keep up even though he is getting very little sleep. He is having difficulty breathing at night. When he dozes off momentarily, his loud snoring keeps others from sleep. In consideration of other pilgrims, he decides to stay in pensiones with a small, private room. The lack of sleep siphons his energy and triggers a need for regular breaks while walking.

At one point, his arm swells up, and he is unable to make a fist. We visit a pharmacy and discover the power of toothpaste which he applies to his arm. Evidently, the same ingredients that polish our teeth soothe several common ailments. Applying a drop of tooth-paste to a bug bite, plant irritant, or insect sting can stop the itching and decrease swelling. When applied to sores or blisters, it dries them up, allowing the wounds to heal.

I'm sleeping fine, but my smaller toes continue to hurt. I'm wearing Smartwool socks that worked so well four years prior. With more experience in footwear, I am using wide shoes a half-size longer than normal to compensate for the natural swelling that comes with so much walking. Although the pain is not severe, it's persistent. I like my shoes tight to avoid blisters but decide that loosening them may help. I have to remind myself daily to resist my tendency for tightness. The pain comes and goes. I had experienced the same sting on the French Camino and is the reason I bought a longer and wider shoe this time.

I love hiking at a good pace, not too casual. When the adrenaline kicks in, I need to move. I really like the idea of walking with my son and am trying to get my pace within his range, and I know he is trying to do the same. So far, it's been hard to slow down. *Are the sore toes a way of slowing me down?* I wonder. We try different walking modes, and my level of discomfort remains. I try to focus on being in the moment with my attention on the intriguing Norte.

Journal entry

Pilgrims seem exceptionally hardy. There is no talk of blisters or miles walked and no competition to claim a bed. The showers are larger than expected, and there are more washing machines than four years prior. We spent the night in an *albergue* with Tim and Tom from Germany, Brendan and his wife from Australia, and a Spanish doctor and his son.

One of the more popular starting points for walking the Norte is Bilbao. Set on the west end of Basque Country, it is the largest city along the Norte. Our route today takes us dead-on into a hustling section of the city that does not appear to value siesta time. In the massive cluster of people, a man spots us from a distance hollering, "Pilgrims, do you need help?" How did he know? He informs us that the *albergue* we seek is a few streets, turns, railroad tracks, and a bridge away. It is impossible to detect the yellow Camino arrows in the busy city, and we rely on a blend of common sense, direction, and those not afraid to yell out.

We finally spot the multistory *albergue* near a small park as we enter a section of the city packed with young black men. They are obviously immigrants in search of jobs and are seemingly not finding them. We see greater human diversity in Bilbao than in other parts of the Norte. The dark skin *albergue* host on the second floor is a recent arrival from Nicaragua who left his country for the same reason as the men outside. He and his wife immigrated with their two children who are now in school. They love Spain but miss their family and lament their children's inability to interact with their grandparents.

After the lengthy day's walk, the first priority is to shower and change into the only set of clean clothes that we own. They are always fresher when I lug them outside my backpack, secured by a pair of gigantic safety pins. At times, I do the same with my sandals to dry them out completely. My son is used to washing as soon as we reach our day's goal, and this time, he leaves on a search for a laundromat. His venture pays off, and we won't need to put clothes out to dry tonight risking that they may still be damp in the morning.

A bit tired by dinnertime, we settle on a sizeable restaurant just below the *albergue* facing the city park. Finding an empty outdoor iron table with matching chairs, we plop ourselves down for the evening. From the vantage point, we can leisurely take in the vigor of city life. Our spirited waitress introduces herself and describes the house specialties and pilgrim favorites. We learn that she is Bolivian, married to a Spaniard and has school-age children in her new home country. She asks a lot of questions about American lifestyles as tomorrow she leaves for Pittsburg, California, to visit her older sister and her family.

After a relatively easy, eighteen-mile Saturday hike, we transition from the beautiful Basque Country that we have enjoyed so much and enter our second autonomous region of Cantabria. Spain has seventeen such regions. Each is an autonomous community (comunidad autónoma)—a first-level political and administrative division.

The regions were created in accord with the Spanish constitution of 1978 for the purpose of guaranteeing and delineating their limited autonomy. At this point, we begin to hear less Basque or Euskara and more Spanish.

Journal entry

Finally, a trying first week is over. It's been hard. Mijo gets very little rest at night making it very difficult to do the long hikes. It was really nice to walk the entire stage with him today. My stomach's been acting up; thankfully, not too serious. I can handle the hikes well and complete a full stage each day. They're a nice challenge.

Late afternoon, we stop for lunch at the Caballo Salto—a beautiful isolated restaurant with floor to ceiling glass windows overlooking the ocean. The site is a pleasant surprise along the way. Sweaty and tired, we feel out of place among nicely dressed tourists. The decision to eat here, however, is made easy by the lack of other facilities. As usual, the staff is gracious and welcoming to tired hikers. Dining with the backpacks by our side, I take out my Camino guidebook which suggests that our day's destination is only a few miles ahead. I am anxious to get a glimpse of where we will spend the weekend, but the immense trees flanking the winding road make it impossible to see beyond them.

My son booked the Agua Viva (Living Water) recommended by the Spanish hiker who helped us get our Russian friend and his dog up the long steps. Agua Viva is in the city of Castro-Urdiales, our next stop after the Caballo Salto. It's where we spend our day of rest. The skimpy Camino guidebook I carry is scarce on details to locate our target as we enter the city. We need more reliable resources. Sensing we may have missed our turn, I flag down a young pedestrian with his dog returning home from a trip to the market. Of course, he can help us, and yes, we just passed the right turnoff. He walks a portion of the path with us on his way home then waves as we part ways.

The Agua Viva is aptly named. It has an indoor heated pool fit for doing laps and an attractively furnished meditation room with burning incense. As we check in, we meet a nice couple on vacation from the US and discover that we are neighbors. Salvador and Cecilia live in Corona. He is curious about our adventure, and over a beer, I fill him in on it. We are all heading west on Monday morning, and he makes a tempting offer to give us a lift to Santander on his rental car. I remind him (really me) that we are committed to walking, sore toes and lethargic from insomnia notwithstanding.

Even though we knew about the ocean along the Norte, I did not think it necessary to pack trunks. On our first full day of rest, it was time to invest. But, being Sunday, finding an open clothing store might not be feasible. The capable Agua Viva receptionist suggests I try the tienda china (Chinese store) where I can "find anything even when other stores are closed." He is right. I buy trunks, disposable shaving razors, and plastic clothes hangers. My wooden hangers from home are starting to fall apart from the strain of wrapping around thick clotheslines. We load up at the tienda china and scout the road we'll be taking Monday morning.

The extensive walks from previous days energized me, and I spend a couple of hours swimming in the pool by myself. Tourist season is over, and we have not seen another pilgrim the entire day. I immerse myself in the serenity of the Camino Norte while Mijo tries to get some sleep. In the evening, we take a short walk to the center of town and find a popular restaurant with indoor and outdoor seating. Having just showered and changed, we pick a table protected from the elements where we can see the large orange sun fading gently behind the ocean.

The assortment of walkers we encounter are mainly from Europe. Most are German, French, and Spanish; some are English and Irish. There are, of course, many countries represented. There is a nice mixture of men and women and of those who came alone or together. Early on, we met a family from Chicago: a father walking with his adult daughter and adult son. He is one of a handful of people about my age, and the Norte may be too much for him. Their plan is to reach Santiago, but we only see them toward the beginning of the trail, and he is struggling.

Monica is happy to be on her own doing the Camino by herself. She is not one drawn to detail planning. "So what moved you to do the Camino?" I asked, and she replies in Spanish, "One day, I put on my hiking gear, locked the front door of my home in Barcelona, and let my phone guide my steps." In her thirties, she had no time to train and intends to walk the entire Camino. She proudly shows us pictures she's taken on her phone while doing leisurely walks. She hauls a big backpack with all kinds of gear and food to get her through each day. Without a guidebook, she uses her phone for information on distance, type of terrain, and availability of facilities on the Camino. She's clearly a very modern pilgrim.

We keep running into four young German friends doing portions of the Camino together. Their English is comprehensible as with many pilgrims we meet. The two girls are walking for two weeks to assess whether to return and do more of the Camino. They know each other from Germany but just met their walking partners. The boys are in it for the long haul. It is a trip they have planned for years and are using vacation time to do the entire Camino. It seems apparent that they will accomplish their goal. One of the guys has a good friend from Chile, and he wears a sombrero gifted to him. It certainly does the trick against the sun, but it's a poor match for rain.

Toward the middle of the second week, one of the German girls is having severe back pains and is ready to stop walking. The other one is feeling strong and stays with her friend. They have no choice but to cut their trip short. We don't see the boys again. Later, other pilgrims tell us that they did not remain on the Camino much longer. Something happened that made them both discontinue their walk.

Two French garçons and a girl walking together have their small dog with them. They are good walkers, and their little dog keeps up although strapped to carry his own food. I notice how cautiously he struts close to them. He does not wander off without purpose. I run into the friendly group in several *albergues*, and it does not seem like the tiny dog is a burden to anyone. In fact, everyone seems to enjoy it. The open space of the Norte seems like a better fit for hikers with dogs, and they seem more prevalent on this Camino. The trio carries phones, and at times, I check with them for Camino information. When we happen to break together, we check in on each other. Eventually, I lose track of them.

Antonio and his wife are a bit older than most walkers but certainly younger than me. This is their first Camino, and they are having a great time. They come from Guadalajara—one of my favorite cities in Mexico. I meet them when walking by myself and stopping to have a soft drink at a coffee shop. He likes to travel and has been to Europe numerous times, but this is a new experience for him. "I love the Camino because it takes me places I would never see as a tourist," he tells me. I know exactly what he means. Except for the larger cities and choice beaches, the rest of the Camino is either not suitable for vehicles or too isolated to be noticed by tourists.

Journal entry

Mijo is resourceful in finding what we need. We avoid the longer coastal hikes and may even seek out streets when they shorten the walking distance. I prefer the more scenic routes. When we walk separately or sleep in different quarters, I miss him. Some pilgrims give me reports of where they've seen him.

Time flies on the Camino. It may be because we are in constant movement, not just with our bodies but our minds as well. Every day, one encounters changes on the Camino, and nothing is like yesterday. When we make new friends, I associate them with a particular town or occasion and part ways not knowing whether I will see them again. Those that we happen to see again, in a different locale, often seem changed. At times, they are walking with different people or alone instead of with others. By the end of the day, the morning seems distant with so much activity in between. A few days are an eternity. Repetition and constancy seem to shorten the days while motion seems to extend time.

Our Sunday stay in Llanes is noisy, although many businesses are closed. The hotel includes a continental breakfast, and I go down while Mijo rests. In the dining area, I run into a couple dozen middle-aged Germans doing a partial Camino for two weeks. They hired a personal guide to lead them and handle their lodging and meal accommodations. They are nicely dressed with many wearing gloves against the increasingly colder weather and couples attired in colorful matching outfits. Their plan is to walk twenty kilometers (about twelve miles) every weekday and hire a van to carry their gear. After I leave, Mijo shows up for breakfast dressed in similar clothes to mine and wearing the required guest name tag. Staff is hesitant to give him access since a guy with the same name was just there.

There is a small beach nearby, and I take a stroll on it. It's a bit cold and not the ideal time to be near water. I have the beach to myself. Mijo stays back at the hotel trying to catch up on some rest. I gather that he just started to see a doctor to help him sleep and will resume consultations when we return home. The streets are pretty full, and church is empty as I make my way in.

At night, the streets are bustling with race car drivers putting on a noisy show for their fans dining outdoors or mingling on the sidewalks. Traffic control is heavy as sporty cars keep circling among the most crowded streets playing loud music and interacting with fans. It's not long before I tire of the racket and make my way to the hotel. Luckily, we are staying across a river and closer to the beach than the raucous section of town.

It is Tuesday in Ribadesella, and we decide to walk at our own pace and schedule. Trying to meet up at day's end without cell phones is not working well for either of us. He really needs to stay in his own room and try to rest while I like the *albergue* experience and walking early. We peruse the map and agree on a location to meet Friday evening. Although our walking plan is not what we anticipated, we adapt. I enjoy doing full stages and the challenge of staying on course and finding needed resources.

I arrive alone in Sebrayo—a tiny village with only one small *albergue*. The fee is just $4 for the bare-bones facility with about a dozen beds. It has no potable water, and there is no restaurant in town! I'm in the middle of nowhere. After the *albergue* host tells the six guests that she is leaving to walk her dog, a couple of pilgrims ask from the street if the *albergue* host is in. When they learn that she's not, they continue walking. I don't think there is another *albergue* nearby, but they leave hastily. While the host is still away, two more pilgrims come by, and each lay claim to a bunk. The paperwork can wait, a different approach.

Once hikers settle in after showering and washing our clothes, we learn of a faucet a block away where we can retrieve our own drinking water. Before dark, a food truck pulls up loaded with a variety of fresh fruits, vegetables, bread, meat, and other treats. My Korean friends are unable to order from the Spanish-speaking vendor, and several of us pitch in. The small kitchen comes in handy tonight for those with cooking skills. I miss my son even more today.

The stage from Sebrayo to Gijon is a robust twenty-two miles—not many free passes on the Norte! The way markings are not clear but manageable. I pass several peregrinos, some much younger. After lunch, on a heavily forested steep climb with no way markings or people around, I'm comforted to see two Polish ladies resting on the side of the path. With my head down and my mind on a tiresome climb, they greet me with "It's beautiful here." I had not realized how much I needed to hear their wake-up call. My mind immediately turns to the surroundings focusing on the positive plainly before me.

The Camino splits at this point. Do we stay on the Norte or veer to the Primitivo? The latter is more mountainous and away from the ocean. I was leaning toward exploring the Primitivo while making our initial plans. My thought was that we would have a chance to build up stamina on the Norte while enjoying the ocean and eventually be ready to try the more demanding inland option. By the time we need to finalize our decision, the Norte has already clarified our best option. Trying another Camino will have to wait.

Journal entry

Today I feel like a pilgrim. My guidebook cautions against the accuracy of the Camino arrows. Even intending to stay on the path can lead me astray. I made several decisions on best guestimates I trusted. Tired upon entering Gijon, the main path splits, and I follow the sign toward the "urban center" for lodging. I guessed wrong! Backtracking cost me an extra couple miles, which seems longer when your body feels you should have arrived.

On my way to Aviles, I run into a Canadian lady who seems disoriented. We are both loading up on fruits starting the morning walk. Her knees are heavily bandaged. Evidently, a doctor on the French Camino advised her to take a bus to Santiago and rest for a week before doing any more walking. She misread a sign and took a bus to Santander putting her on a more difficult Camino which she is determined to walk. Call me crazy.

On a chilling and soggy afternoon in Novellana, we are relieved to reach a cozy restaurant for lunch by a small paved road with the ocean behind it. About to enter, we notice Antonio and his wife fighting their way against a strong wind to the next town, still five miles away. They see us and seem at once determined to continue and enticed to stop. Reason prevails and soaking wet, they join us at a large wooden table by a fireplace burning natural wood. It is surely a perfect time for wine. My son and I are spending the night here and invite them to break with us. I could not fathom leaving the fireplace and was taken back by their resolve to continue walking after lunch. It was the last time we saw them.

Novellana is a tiny close-knit town with a few basic facilities. The old church next door is unlocked once a week for an hour by a traveling priest. The small café mirrors a familiar scene of local men watching soccer and chatting. They are the best source of information for pilgrims. Coming into town, we don't see any signs of a laundromat. This may be one of those places where we wash in a sink and hang clothes to dry in our room. We wait for a commercial to interrupt and learn that the town's gas station has a washing machine. While my son does that chore, I inquire about a market to stock up on fruits. A man points across the street lined with scattered homes saying, "That's a store, just knock." I am not usually skeptical but find myself looking for signs between them for the real message.

After a few knocks at the designated home, I am about to leave when the door is pulled ajar revealing a small, shadowy room. I am still not convinced until my eyes adjust to the dark, and I make out scattered cans, fruit baskets, and paper goods. A nice elderly couple run the place, which I imagine is their primary source of income. The woman, having read my face, explains that it is too expensive to put up a store sign, and they rely on neighbors to guide visitors. In the lighter background, I see a variety of trees and realize that I am getting fruit from the vine. They seem pleased to receive a customer who obviously buys more than needed.

Time and movement on the Camino seem to amplify everything and awaken the unconscious. Each step toward Santiago is special: one we've never taken before—one that countless pilgrims from throughout the world took, each with his own motive. Deep thoughts arise, seemingly unprovoked, giving life to new dreams and inspiring growth. Our existence becomes less vague as the push to walk five hundred miles clears mental webs. It is the perfect environment (retreat) to invoke fundamental questions of identity and purpose and the right setting to take stock of one's journey in life. Occasionally, I find myself abruptly visited by thoughts long cast aside but, evidently, not entirely gone. At times, they come in dreams feeling like a cleansing shower.

Journal entry

Today's reading seems particularly applicable, "The Lord's will is accomplished... Let your mercy be on us as I place my trust in you." Each day, I walk without any real knowledge of where I am going, what the weather will be, and if I will arrive safely or at all. Will I find food on time and stay healthy? I can struggle with questions I cannot answer or accept the invitation to let go of the illusion that I am in control and enjoy the journey. The personal choice determines my state of mind.

The powerful common pursuit of walking toward Santiago bonds pilgrims regardless of language, country of origin, or any other distinction. Connections are genuine even though every greeting is a probable goodbye. Perhaps that is why both are expressed with only one phrase, "Buen Camino." The expression is loaded with meaning and shared freely. If indeed the Camino is a metaphor for life, the words express eternal good wishes not only for the moment of mutual exchange but also for every step thereafter. Latin American countries use the term, "Vaya con Dios" to express a similar sentiment.

People on the Camino put themselves in a position of high impact. It is not an experience to take lightly although some will try.

People travel long distances to walk in unfamiliar land for a variety of reasons. Some connect their faith to the Camino seeing it as a religious experience—a sort of spiritual retreat. Others may start off without clear purpose and find something meaningful revealed to them, perhaps even in spite of themselves. For all, it is an undeniable adventure. Regardless of one's own goals or expectations, people are not left untouched by the journey in a positive way, even if not readily grasped. The Camino is not *Fantasy Island*. Things are bound to happen that derail our comfortable assumptions, and thus, it is ours to recognize that the bigger challenges are really our best teachers.

After a water break on the outskirts of a farming town, I encourage my son to continue ahead while I journal in silence under a large fig tree overlooking the little village. Busy writing, I don't mind his direction. When I leave, shortly thereafter, I cannot find him. My mind races to make sense of why I am unable to catch up to him. In concern, random questions pop into my head. Did I pass him on an isolated road? Did he take a fall somewhere and I missed him?

After some futile searching, I flag down a local woman with a cell phone. We try calling my son, but he has no local phone service. She calls the Guardia Civil (local police) for me. The officer drives out to meet me and takes a description of my son. He asks that I wait as he goes out to find him. Before long, he returns with bad news. No one has seen him. I thank the officer and the woman and continue walking somberly. I'm in a town now and finding him will get harder.

Suddenly, the officer reappears and gives me a ride to where I last saw my son. Behind some branches, I see a yellow Camino arrow pointing in a different direction than the one I took. The source of confusion is cleared up, and the officer gives me a lift until we reach the end of his jurisdiction. After a short walk, I spot Mijo waiting for me by the roadside. He probably thinks I had a lot to journal.

Generally, people treat the Camino with reverence, taking care of it and each other. It is most noticeable on the Norte where we never see discarded paper that too often taints rural portions of the Frances. On the contrary, we see trash receptacles everywhere.

Spaniards make safety a top priority, and pilgrims benefit from very affordable medical care as well as police protection. The last time my son walked into a hospital without showing proof of medical insurance and received medical treatment without payment was not in the US. Neither was the time that a police officer came to help me out of a jam caused by my own negligence and then gives me a ride so that I can remedy my problem.

Spaniards are very active people with a strong presence on the Norte. It is an endearing feature. They appear everywhere like gracious hosts ready to share their knowledge. Even if they are only out for a walk, as many often are, they readily pause to provide assistance. We see it frequently while walking and even when we stop to rest. Whenever the opportunity shows up, I try to connect with them. They enrich my time on the Camino and give greater meaning to my surroundings. Yet I notice that they do not impose themselves. Recognizing people's needs to experience the Camino their own way, Spaniards are not apt to interfere in any way or be disruptive.

On a dark, gloomy day, we cross a good-sized river and get drenched by a hefty storm. The dense rain impairs our vision, and we are unable to see anything that might protect us from the elements. Unable to talk or hear each other against the shivering wind and pounding rain, we set our heads down fighting to keep our balance. I glance wistfully on a big farmhouse that I am barely able to make out in the heavy downpour, although the house is nearby. In our wanting state, it looks like a mirage: too good to be real. In a moment of timely compassion, we reach an old bus stop structure completely open a foot above ground and covered with spider webs. This one we can claim! We are able to temporarily escape the pouring rain and catch our breath. It is an interval of temporary relief, and we savor it before being forced to face our circumstance and get to our destination.

We keep trying to adjust our walking pace in order to continue walking together. Mijo is getting very little sleep at night and needs to move slowly and break often. After a while, we both realize that we need to adapt differently. I walk ahead, and we meet at the end of the day. It is much easier on both of us to walk at our own pace. I wait for Mijo before entering a town to make it easier to find each other. As pilgrims arrive, I inquire about my son's whereabouts. The ones who saw him immediately make the connection since we wear similar clothes, sport beards, and are the only non-native Latinos on the Norte.

Meeting at the end of each hike creates new challenges. What if he needs to stop for the night before reaching me? He has no way to inform me of his decision and feels pressed to continue walking. Similarly, my ability to maintain movement is limited to staying at my post waiting for him in irregular weather conditions, at times without shelter. We fine tune our plan and resort to meeting after numerous hikes. Once we consult my guidebook to find the most convenient place to meet, he notes it on his phone and writes it down on the guidebook. It is not the plan we had envisioned and certainly not the one we planned so methodically. How often do we have the final say on how our lives ought to be or for how long? Learning to adapt is crucial and necessary even if painful and disappointing. Mijo had no problem tweaking and neither did I. Ultimately, the new strategy works well physically but illustrates how shared miseries are halved and shared happiness is doubled.

On my own on a nice sunny morning, I notice a local man about my age walking briskly ahead of me. Rather than passing by with the customary Buen Camino greeting, I check to see if he feels like having company. For about ten kilometers (he does fifteen daily), we walk together in pleasant conversation. Retirement has given him more quality time for contemplation and walking. He is uneasy and hopeful about the future and worries about the impact of technology on human interaction. As I listen to him, I keep hearing my own hopes and apprehensions mirrored by this total stranger in rural Spain.

Tired and hungry, I finally reach the city's congested central plaza. I am not in a mood for crowds and stand looking around for an escape route. From a set of stairs, a local man catches my eye. He seems to be on the lookout for lost pilgrims. I decide to approach him as he seems like someone who can explain the sign I just passed referencing two Camino paths out of town. He is happy to help me and suggests that I take the more scenic track, although it is longer. He enquires about my ancestry, and I explain that I am his distant, half brother fathered by Hernán Cortez. As we say our goodbyes, he gives me a heartfelt welcome to Spain and offers his prayers that I make my way back to the motherland.

Following the yellow Camino arrows, I feel like I'm alternating directions: at times toward Santiago and then away from it. The sun is a dead giveaway that I am lost. My guidebook cautions against misleading way markings in the area but provides no helpful alternatives. As frustration with the unreliable waymarks grows, I eventually find a more familiar sign leading me back to a previous location. I am not thrilled to backtrack but trust that it is a necessary correction. On the right path now, I realize that drifting cost me about seven miles, and my stomach demands retribution.

The mind responds powerfully to finding my way, and I plow ahead with fresh vigor at my changing fate. "Thank you, Jesus!" I scream. Before long, however, my excitement reverts to irritation at those who would post confusing road signs. This time, I voice my displeasure out loud to the wind, "Maldecidos," (roughly, "Thoughtless") I yell. When alone, there is a lot of room for self-talk and shifting moods.

Journal entry

I have never walked against such powerful wind before. Broken eucalyptus branches lie everywhere. I am forced to remove the hearing aids and take extra care not to trip over my flying poles, which at the same time help keep my balance. They picked the right place for so many wind turbines.

In this state of mind, I spot a local man standing in the middle of a desolate paved road, miles from town. He holds a long narrow stick in one hand, and I notice a worn-out bucket nearby. I greet him, and he seems quite attentive. Perfect! I figure he is my only chance to express my anger at whoever posted the wicked way markings.

The man is an expert at deflating anger; he is attentive, straight-faced, and completely quiet. I can feel that he is not impressed by my outburst, and his calm demeanor enables me to recover my senses. Suddenly, I stand paralyzed facing him, grateful for him and for so much more, and realize I have no idea what this man's own situation might be. We never really talk. I wonder how often he gathers walnuts, how far he walks to do so, and what he does with them. I start to leave, and he invites me to his stash. Sheepishly, I take a couple for the road and say adios.

Alone, I have walked only about eleven miles and am set on doing another eight today mainly because my book shows the next *albergue* there but also because my mind is programmed to keep going in spite of the rain. To my surprise, I am facing a brand new *albergue* just open. I hesitate a bit but decide to spend the night. The small *albergue* has a dozen beds and half are twice the standard Camino size. I waver to claim a big bed that two people might use, but the host suggests that it won't be a problem. He hands me my own adjustable, portable heater and shows me the nice big showers and washing machines. It's a real treat to shower leisurely, wash, and hang my clothes to dry without any hurry as no one else has checked in. In the afternoon and evening, I see familiar faces pass by in the rain, and I'm puzzled as to why no one stops. I suspect the internet is the source of their decision to keep walking, and I don't know what to make of that.

The curious *albergue* is family-owned, and the little restaurant next to it is also theirs. They open for supper around 8:00 p.m., and I head over in the chilling wind. The *albergue* host is tending bar as several men huddle close for soccer and drinks. I am the only *albergue* patron, and it is evident that I am the only visitor in this group as well—a privilege circumstance on a cold, wet night, I tell myself. I request a key from the host to lock the *albergue* for the night and sleep like a baby in my own private quarters. I opt for breakfast before leaving and have a chance to thank the host's mom for the tasty ribs the previous meal.

Today, we walk together and decide to deviate from the Camino to reduce the walking distance. Finding our way around the streets in Castropol is convoluted and so is finding lodging. We reach out for help and find vacancy in a hotel next to a wide river. The next morning, we learn that the ferry season is ended. Walking across a huge bridge in heavy traffic is not a good option, and we miss the city bus. We settle on having a taxi take us to Ribadeo across the river dropping us off on the Camino path. I should be grateful, but a much stronger longing takes over. In the drizzling, cold wind, it is the only time on the Camino that I feel like finding a warm place to hide myself and avoid walking. I don't share my temporary insanity with Mijo fearing we might talk each other into slacking off.

As I walk briskly to keep warm, we lose complete sight of each other. The paths are long, and as the rain subsides, I am faced with beautiful scenes of rolling hills, rich soil, and enormous trees. The area is strikingly picturesque, and I feel envious of those who live in the paradise that I get to walk on. There are scarce buildings along the path except for random weather-worn farm structures. To my surprise, as I climb a gradual hill, there stands a small coffee shop where a few pilgrims gather to catch their breath and the peaceful scenery. I take my hot café americano outside and join a young French man on the only tiny outdoor table.

He is doing the Norte on his own and loves it. Like others I meet, he first walked the French Camino and offers a graphic description of his impression. "I did not like seeing mostly peoples' butts instead of nature, and there were far too many businesses along the way." Wow! That's an exceptionally harsh assessment. Other pilgrims who had walked the two Caminos shared many positive experiences from both. The constant differentials shared are crowd size and all that entails, the ocean, and level of difficulty. Not everyone prefers the cooler weather of the Norte.

Before leaving the café, I chat with the kind lady running the café from behind the counter explaining that my son is on the Camino with me, and I'm sure will stop soon at her café. "You can't miss him; he's a big man who looks like me." I ask if I can leave a note for him and she agrees to give it to him. "Mijo, enjoy this restful place. See you this evening." He got my note.

Journal entry

I am not walking much in darkness but still need to use my rain jacket to keep warm. It rains less than I had anticipated, but coming from a dry area, it is much more than what I am used to. I no longer see people my age on the Camino. Almost all or our friends from the beginning stages have disappeared. Occasionally, we meet someone from the past who has news of their own or of others we came to know briefly.

Everyone makes adjustments on the Camino by need or desire and the original schedules normally serve only as broad frameworks. Some people cut down on walking when the rain hits hard to avoid injury. Others skip stages that they deem too difficult, or they choose to spend extra time in special places. There are several world-renowned sites easily accessible from the Camino that some pilgrims choose to visit. One such place is the Altamira Cave famous for its prehistoric paintings and engravings near the historic town of Santillana del Mar just west of Santander. It is not a major detour from the Norte, but we decide to continue walking. We pretty much keep on the Camino, and whatever sightseeing we do comes once we reach Santiago and are able to rent a car.

It was our desire not to separate the last few stages and arrive in Santiago together. We made several attempts but were not able to sustain them to our final destination. Like other plans we made, this one too did not conform to our expectations but rather birthed something new. An old question comes back to me. Are you leaving room for surprises? I wonder what the Camino would be if all our plans went according to our desires. How realistic is that expectation, and is it really something we want? Whether on the Camino or anywhere else, we deal with what comes; we try our best to adapt, and it shapes us. It is the only way growth comes to us. Whether we cooperate with change or go kicking and screaming is the only decision we get to make.

The last remaining stages are much easier than the ones at the beginning, and it is not only due to conditioning. Stages are rated on a scale from one to five with one being the easiest. The entire first week consisted only of levels five and four. They all seemed like fives to me. This week, they are every other rating, except the top two. The levels of difficulty seem backwards for convenience's sake, but the Camino is not about comfort.

Gontan is a tiny town with one $6 *albergue*. The stage to reach Gontan is hard, and I arrive drained, sweaty, and hungry. Completing the stage was not a sure thing with the hard wind pushing against me. I worry needlessly about my son doing a similar hike by himself and am comforted by the thought that he carries a phone and can communicate in Spanish. We walk separately for the third consecutive day, and I resume using my headlamp for the early predawn hikes.

I much prefer reaching *albergues* in daylight and not being preoccupied with finding Camino signs to guide me in the dark. Gontan's little *albergue* lacks nothing that I need, and I sleep like a tired baby.

Not carrying a phone over forty days is a rare treat for me. Doing so for five hundred miles in unknown country makes it a real adventure. When I'm by myself, I don't know the time and must rely on the sun—when I can see it. My guidebook does not provide names for every small town, and there are times when I don't know where I stand. This kind of freedom can be alarming, but it need not be. It is only uncomfortable because we've grown used to having phones as an extension of our bodies. Relying on one's own intuition and awareness for vital information and turning to each other for assistance is refreshing. I never want to do a virtual Camino.

In Sobrado, I reach the famous tenth century Monasterio de Santa Maria an hour before siesta ends and the reopening of the massive wooden doors. I wait in the spacious courtyard as others, mostly tourists, begin to arrive. Pilgrims are welcome to spend the night for $6 and use the showers and washing machines. After participating in the monastery's traditional evening Vespers, I head out to what seems the most popular restaurant among several nearby. As I walk in, a group of French and English pilgrims invite me to join them for supper, which has a feel of an end-of-Camino celebration. People are processing the effects of the Camino recounting their most vivid incidents which always include other pilgrims. Before making my way back to the ancient monasterio, I walk silently in semidarkness to mail my second set of postcards.

Mijo and I are only twenty-five miles from Santiago among a French Camino crowd after the two Caminos merge. Actually, at this point, people who walk one hundred kilometers from Sarria to Santiago are in the mix as well. It is a loud mass of pilgrims. Mijo's back is hurting, and he insists that I continue on without him. I take his camera to carry the rest of the way, and he writes on my guidebook the address of our rendezvous in Santiago where he made reservations. At this point, he is no longer staying in *albergues* as not to disrupt others from sleep.

I'm less than ten kilometers from the cathedral when the heavens open up fiercely. *Some welcome*, I tell myself. Luckily, I find refuge in a restaurant and take my time with a cup of coffee that keeps my hands warm. After several refills, the waiter tries to discourage me from resuming my walk, and I keep thinking that it can't rain that hard that long.

This time, I don't feel the sadness and the joy of reaching Santiago from four years prior, and the sun is not shining as it was then. My gloom comes from not being able to walk the final stage with my son. Yet knowing that he is where he needs to be and so am I. He is healing, and I am soaking wet and loving it. The Norte shredded my agenda from day one when I misbooked a flight and took a train instead from Barcelona to San Sebastian. My carefully laid plans and wishes were cast aside for something different from what I would ever choose. It made the Norte much more than I expected and, in many ways, felt like being on a Camino for the first time. It was just like the amazing retreat that you attend unable to imagine a better one only to find the next one equally satisfying and refreshing and different.

Finisterre and Home

—— ❧ ——

From the Hotel Universal in Plaza Galicia, over the roofs of buildings in between, we can see the Cathedral de Santiago. By the time I arrive soaking wet, Mijo is already registered and resting. A little later, over dinner in Santiago, we talk about our next steps. Mijo has a doctor's appointment tomorrow, and we agree to meet in Finisterre (end of the world) in three days. The following morning, I start my walk toward the cathedral plaza. It is October 18, and the weather has gotten colder. The dark streets glisten with the night's moisture from the glow of uneven city lights. I'm not sure to see the sun today. The yellow Camino arrows leading out of the city toward the Atlantic Ocean are in a part of the plaza that I had only seen from a distance, and it takes me a moment to find them. Eventually, I begin to see hikers on the Camino; not many, but there are still more than on the Norte. I want to take my time now that my walking in Spain is coming to an end but am mindful of covering almost one hundred kilometers in three stages.

I learn that the first stage on the Camino Finisterre is rated a five in level of difficulty and chuckle to myself. It feels very much like a one on the Norte. I am further amused to leave my son with only an agreement to meet in Finisterre in three days. The city is large, and I have no phone or car, not even a map. Normally, I am wired for more specific details. This is not my usual pattern, and it feels great. The Camino is having an impact!

Once dawn breaks, I catch up with a couple of men walking the Camino and join them. The Irish and Spanish pair have just met and have strange plans of doing a "Quemada" pagan ritual when they reach Muxia. It's not clear to me what they have in mind and lack the curiosity to ask. Both have been walking portions of the French Camino over the years in two-week intervals. A bit later, I stop for coffee, and we part ways.

I'm enjoying the fairly easy hike and consider walking beyond the day's goal. When I ask people about facilities, should I continue to walk, I get unreliable information and decide to keep to the schedule. During lunch the next day, a waitress gives me a free colorful map of the Camino Finisterre with plenty of details. She won't accept a donation. "It's a service we provide" she tells me.

The night before my last hike to Finisterre, I lay awake in Oliveira, unable to sleep for long. I have no idea of the time. I peek outside for clues and find none. Too many thoughts fill my mind from many directions. Mostly, I am so grateful for the Camino experience with my son. His flexibility and independence allowed me to walk the entire Camino. How he hung in there the entire time is amazing to me, given the challenges he confronted. In his shoes, I may have packed my few belongings and gone home. I'm glad he does not give up easily.

I leave early on my final hike and by midafternoon make my way to the beach in Finisterre. It's my last chance to remove my boots and soak my worn-out feet. My small toes are not completely pain-free and will take time to heal. Around me I notice perfectly shaped scallop shells and I retrieve them as others have done for centuries. I return to the main trail and continue walking not knowing exactly where the road ends. Now I begin to wonder where I may see Mijo. Nearing my final destination, I see the rotunda where we took a picture with Brad and Cathy four years prior. I look around, half-expecting to see my son, but he is not here. It's the only place I know to look for him, and I keep walking.

It's a short uphill walk to the lighthouse at the tip of Cape Finisterre overlooking the Atlantic Ocean with a Camino sign below showing zero miles left on the journey. On my way up, I stop at what remains of the Santa Maria de Fisterra church with a chapel of Santo Cristo. For centuries, it has been the traditional site to pause and offer thanksgiving upon completing the Camino. As I resume the last remaining steps, walking alongside a busy thoroughfare, I begin to see groups of tourists, merchants, and a few pilgrims. It's a busy place with a mixture of itineraries. My body suddenly informs me that someone is watching me. I slow down pausing to scan my surrounding and am elated to spot Mijo parked in a car across a busy street with his camera toward me.

It is an amazing occasion to complete the entire Camino in one piece and finally unload the baggage I've been hauling on my back for over five hundred miles. At first chance, I could not unload my poles and backpack into the trunk of the car and shut it tight fast enough. Finally, Mijo and I are ready to explore Finisterre by car. My hiking clothes may give me away, but with a radio, a heater, and sandals, I begin to feel like a tourist.

From Finisterre, Mijo drives to Muxia where we spent time relaxing on enormous boulders overlooking the ocean and enjoying the interplay between the crashing waves and land. It is the perfect first stop from Finisterre and a fitting way to part the ocean as we make our way inland.

That evening, we decide to revisit a bar from four years prior in Santiago. I'm done with hiking shoes and opt for sandals on the cold cobblestone streets. After some futile attempts, the numerous small streets start to look the same, and I give up trying to find it. Mijo's sense of direction and persistence are better than mine. Soon we're climbing familiar steps to a small place run by a nephew-look-alike with great drinks, snacks, and American rock and roll. It is as near as we get to a homecoming celebration and phasing into a different mindset.

The next day, we rise early for coffee while most of Santiago sleeps. With only a few days left before our departure from Barcelona, we just need to attend the Pilgrim Mass at the Catedral de Santiago and get our Compostela (certificate of completion) before making our way across northern Spain all the way east. Mass is not until noon, and we recall that the lines for the Compostela get awfully long. With almost one thousand pilgrims arriving in Santiago daily, we do not want to spend hours waiting in line, not after being constantly on the move.

In predawn, we make our way to the building for our certificate with only one person already in line. Somehow, waiting in sandals on a cold street without light does not seem abnormal. As we casually walk in to receive our Compostela, we learn that we are among ten pilgrims invited to a free lunch at the famous Hotel de Los Reyes

Católicos. On my pilgrim's budget and attire, I had not considered having lunch at the beautiful and very expensive hotel.

The popular pilgrim's mass at the cathedral looks like a gathering of the United Nations. Everyone seems full of life and excited to be there. Many are taking pictures to remember the special occasion. Mijo and I arrive early while there is still ample room and good seats to the altar and the famous botafumeiro that fills the entire cathedral with large quantities of burning frankincense. Confessions are taking place before mass in a variety of languages posted outside each confessional. What a great opportunity to conclude the Camino experience with a final confession in the famous cathedral with the remains of St. James. After all, it was this final destination of the Camino that drew us to Spain weeks ago full of hope and expectations and wonderment.

When mass ends at 1:00 p.m., we rush to the nearby Hotel de Los Reyes Católicos for our much-anticipated lunch. A long table is set for ten lucky pilgrims, and the waiter is taking orders as we arrive. We settle on English as the common language as our new friends from around the globe share highlights and memories of their Camino adventure. Not all of us walked the same Camino and even those who did are enriched by how others process their experiences differently.

After lunch, we leisurely stroll around the cathedral one last time but without lugging our backpacks or wearing hiking shoes. It is fairly packed with a nice mixture of groups of tourists, Spanish families, and a few scattered pilgrims like us. Mijo is taking pictures, and we are but a few feet apart among the crowd. From a cluster of tourists, a lady suddenly runs toward me kissing me on the cheek and asking me if Mijo is alright. I had not recognized her without her Camino gear, but she remembered my waiting around on the trails asking pilgrims if they had seen him.

With no great hurry to reach Barcelona, we leave Santiago in late afternoon. The roads are in great condition, and with Mijo's experience driving in Spain, we make good progress stopping for supper in Leon. Mijo recognizes places we visited when we walked through the beautiful city four years earlier. He had taken pictures of the Cathedral's elaborate architecture and pointed stained windows. With half a tank of gas left even after driving midpoint across Spain, we spend the night in Burgos where, four years prior, a couple had welcomed us into their home for home cooking and rest. We start the next day making our way unhurriedly through beautiful country until reaching Zaragoza— the capital of Spain's Aragon region where we rest and share a meal.

Mijo found a nice and conveniently located hotel in Barcelona where we spent our final three nights. The hotel is near the beach and close to the metro station and several major shopping areas. We still have the rental car and make our way to the popular Sagrada Familia Basilica along with busloads of tourists. The site is not far from the hotel, and I half-tease that I will walk back. Having gained a new appreciation for the ocean and with the beach nearby, we walk there on our first break for a late breakfast. Afterward, Mijo walks back to the hotel to rest, and I stay behind in the fresh ocean breeze and easy sun rays. The ocean helps me transition unhurriedly from the Camino, and I find myself returning to it and thinking about biking to the beach when I get home.

Our central location is so convenient that we have no further need for a car and decide to return it early to the airport. Finding a way to get there to catch our flight from the hotel will not be a problem. The more interesting issue is making our way back to the hotel from the airport. As it turns out, we find several alternative means to get to know the city. Once we drop off the car, we board a comfortable bus for Barcelona which still leaves us a good distance from the hotel, and we are not much into walking at this point. Looking around, we decide to do what locals do and use the metro that takes us nearer our destination yet not quite there. We are now close enough to disregard the taxi option and walk a little. We found many ways to travel in Spain, although our feet did most of the work as the Camino did its work on us.

Conclusion

⸺ ✑ ⸺

A week before departing for the North Camino, my three most pressing questions were, "Am I adequately prepared?" "Will it rain a lot?" "Is this Camino a good choice?" Yes, I was adequately prepared, physically. It was challenging, but no aspect of it was overly demanding. The issues I had with my toes and stomach were not severe and are a key part of what a Camino entails. When you journey out, there will always be some suffering that need not diminish the experience and, in fact, enriches it. Realistically, there were times when we walked more than was necessary, given the number of days allowed for the entire Camino. I am not very skilled at walking at a pace far different from my own and failed miserably at it.

Spiritually, the plan to contemplate scripture daily and do the examen weekly worked well as did taking a little more substantial journal than my previous Camino. Obviously, reading scripture in the morning while walking does not work in the rain. I had to adjust the schedule and sometimes forgot to incorporate the readings into the day. From my previous Camino experience, I knew that churches are often locked and without a priest to celebrate mass. I was able, however, to attend some masses (one in Euskara another in Latin) and do reconciliation. Staying in monasteries or other religious alternatives supports various spiritual goals. I would highly recommend walking the Camino without a cell phone, if that is at all possible as a way to detach from distractions and be fully present to the Camino.

My apprehension of having to walk on slippery ground was mostly unfounded. While it happens, it is not the norm. I expected more rain and am happy that it rained on us only about nine days while walking, a couple of times quite heavily as the day I reached Santiago. Most rain fell at night, and it was not unusual to have to negotiate puddles on our path the next day. On the plus side, the cool weather made walking less laborious. While I scotch guarded my rain jacket, the pockets were still somewhat vulnerable. However, the airtight plastic bags we used to protect our important documents did the trick. I wore hiking shoes rather than boots, and they were suitable for the weather conditions even around puddles. I prefer the ease of carrying and wearing a rain jacket (with a hood) to the bulkiness of a poncho and its clumsiness in heavy winds. At times, my clean clothes did not completely dry overnight, and I attached them outside my backpack for the sun to dry the next day.

The North Camino was extremely satisfying, albeit unpredictable. It offers pilgrims much better opportunities to be alone and thus be more vulnerable and receptive to the surroundings. The senses become sharper and stimulate veiled thoughts and emotions. It is an ideal monthlong moving retreat enriched by both mountains and water. I am not a big fan of water sports nor spend much time on the beach. Yet I found walking on the moist sand, along with the vast ocean views of the Norte, extremely soothing. While the Norte makes you work a little harder, it is not disproportionate to its generous rewards. The Norte, more than the Frances, offers the solitude and silence needed to truly hear, see, and feel something greater than oneself.

Like other pilgrims who shared their observations, I am glad to have walked the French Camino first and that I got the chance to experience the Norte afterward. It feels like a natural sequence transitioning from an urban home environment filled with noise and distractions to the French Camino to gain some experience and confidence and finally tackle the more demanding North Camino. Yet there is room for all manner of individual creativity. Who can know what is best for someone else or even for oneself? Besides, the Camino is about leaving room for surprises.

Dad's Camino Experience

ℐ

I've never been a hiker. When I was first invited to walk the Camino, my biggest concern was my physical preparedness. My doctor was reassuring, and my confidence grew by meeting people who had walked it. I was aware of my need to train hard and had the time and access to demanding terrain. Walking with a full backpack matching the distance of the daily Camino hikes paid off. I never got blisters or suffered injuries in Spain.

The awareness of the long and intricate history of the Camino and those who walked it before me in much harsher conditions influenced me to travel lightly and reverently. It entailed leaving technology at home, walking the entire way carrying my own backpack, and staying in inexpensive, bare-bones *albergues* (exceptions on the North Camino). It is a cleansing experience particularly for those of us who hold on to more than we need.

I found it vastly liberating relying on my own two feet to carry all my essential belongings not knowing exactly where to eat or sleep each night and being on the same path that countless others have taken over hundreds of years. I was truly amazed at how well my body and mind responded to the demands of the Camino and at the satisfaction derived from giving myself the freedom to stretch.

Spain is a welcoming nation and offers pilgrims all the support needed. Public safety is not an issue, and both fellow pilgrims and hosts gladly offer any assistance requested. All of the essentials are provided, and pilgrim can freely choose the type of Camino they wish to experience. Without technology, I got lost a few times. It gave me more reason to interact with the locals who invariably showed great kindness ("Here, I'll walk you to where I'm pointing.").

Before my second Camino, I became a practicing spiritual director and completed the St. Ignatius Exercises. On the Camino Norte, I was more focused on daily prayer, contemplation, and journaling. I created my own acronym for being more intentional: MAP (mindful, attentive, present). The Norte was much more demanding and less predictable. It really helped me to be less rigid and more flexible. In that regard, I was very fortunate to have first walked the French Camino.

Since I started hiking, I have done as many miles at home as on the Camino. I love walking and find it mystifyingly therapeutic. It is truly a gift of time to contemplate, to be alone with my thoughts, and to listen without constant noise and interruptions. Long walks make it easier to surrender the individual will, abandon the ego, and let God lead the way.

Son's Camino Experience

———— ⟋⟍ ————

Hands down, two of the best traveling adventures of my life. I am both humbled and grateful to have made these journeys with my dad. Not only is my dad the perfect mentor guide and traveling partner through life but he also commands one heck of a Camino. In preparation, he mountain-hiked fourteen miles a day during brutal Yorba, Linda, and Chino Hills summers. I joined him on a handful of those hikes, and those were some great times too.

I did my Camino with a camera and the intention to share it all from my lens' perspective. I was ready to capture what walking five hundred hundred miles across Spain in thirty days, with only a backpack of essentials and a camera, looked like to me.

The routine of a day was to wake up at 4:50 a.m., clean your bedding area, brush your teeth, put on your gear, and set out walking in darkness with only a headlamp to light your way until the sun became bright enough to see the road.

Every day was a scenic hike through the history of one of the richest cultures in the world. Completing each hiking day was the best feeling of accomplishment. It was celebrated with a shower, washing our clothes, exploring to find a meal, and resting to do it all again the next day in a different part of the Camino. The comradery grew every day as pelegrinos knew we were all sharing an incredible journey.

About the Author

Ruben did not start hiking until a couple of months before doing the initial Camino de Santiago at the age of sixty-eight. His entire career was in education with the last twenty years in the district office as deputy superintendent of schools, not exactly physically demanding.

Walking the Camino with his son, Ruben Daniel, was unlike any other shared experience including a week in a horse ranch in Wyoming. Without the full support of his wife, Socorro, none of the father-son adventures would be possible.

A year prior to the printing of this book, Ruben Daniel became a first-time dad. He, Jill, and their daughter, Breya, live in Los Angeles.

CPSIA information can be obtained
at www.ICGtesting.com
Printed in the USA
BVHW090356311021
620275BV00005B/112